Connecticut Lore
Strange, Off-Kilter, and Full of Surprises

Zachary Lamothe

Schiffer Publishing Ltd

4880 Lower Valley Road • Atglen, PA 19310

In Memory of

Elizabeth "Gaggi" Lalla, whose stories were the inspiration for this book.

Dedication

To my mom, dad, and my fiancée who provided me immeasurable help throughout the whole process.

Acknowledgments

**Killingly Historical Society
East Haddam Historical Society
Homer D. Babbidge Library at the
University of Connecticut
Woodstock Public Library
Connecticut Civilian Conservation
Corps Museum
Gillette Castle State Park**

Schiffer Books are available at special discounts for bulk purchases for sales promotions or premiums. Special editions, including personalized covers, corporate imprints, and excerpts can be created in large quantities for special needs. For more information contact the publisher:

Published by Schiffer Publishing, Ltd.
4880 Lower Valley Road
Atglen, PA 19310
Phone: (610) 593-1777; Fax: (610) 593-2002
E-mail: Info@schifferbooks.com.

For the largest selection of fine reference books on this and related subjects, please visit our website at
www.schifferbooks.com.
We are always looking for people to write books on new and related subjects. If you have an idea for a book, please contact us at
proposals@schifferbooks.com.

This book may be purchased from the publisher.
Please try your bookstore first.
You may write for a free catalog.

In Europe, Schiffer books are distributed by
Bushwood Books
6 Marksbury Ave.
Kew Gardens
Surrey TW9 4JF England
Phone: 44 (0) 20 8392 8585; Fax: 44 (0) 20 8392 9876
E-mail: info@bushwoodbooks.co.uk
Website: www.bushwoodbooks.co.uk

Designed by Mark David Bowyer
Type set in Bard / Book Antiqua

ISBN: 978-0-7643-4315-5
Printed in the United States of America

Special Thanks

To Dinah Roseberry, my editor—the publication of this book would have been impossible without her.

To my parents, Ken and Linda Lamothe, who spent much time brainstorming with me, visiting places, and editing my work.

To Jaclyn Raffol, who read the first drafts of this work and had to put up with me through this process.

To David Halperin who showed me the ropes on how to put a book together in the first place.

To the following people and organizations who gave me leads for stories, supplied me with crucial information, or had a story to share: the staff at the Killingly Historical Society, Professor Bill Dopirak, Dr. Morgan Martin, Len Grayek, Elizabeth "Gaggi" Lalla, the staff at the Brooklyn Historical Society, Andrew Heist, James Wheeler, Lauren Coletti, Adam Coletti, Michelle Laprade at the Woodstock Library, Katie Burritt, Sarah and Emily Destefano, Diana Silva, the staff at the CCC Museum, the staff at New Haven's Center Church, Dan Salem and Ashley Kumer, the staff at the East Haddam Historical Society, Natalie Coolidge from the Killingly Historical Society, Laurie Knitter, Pat Green, Jeanne Foley and Faith Borger, and Kathryn Lamagna.

A special thanks to Jaclyn Raffol, Mom and Dad, Luke Serwinski, Katie Burritt, Jim Wheeler, and Craig Murphy for accompanying me on my journeys traversing the state.

Contents

Section 1
Abandoned
and Forgotten

A stone chamber at Gungywamp that can be used as a calendar.

1.
Moodus Oddities
Location: East Haddam

For a small rural Connecticut town, East Haddam has its share of curious places, in addition to its more well known attractions of Gillette Castle and Devil's Hopyard State Park. There is an abandoned living-history style museum called Johnsonville: there are abandoned resorts; and in the Moodus section of town, one can hear rumblings reverberating from the underground.

Johnsonville

Nestled between Routes 151 and 149 is the "town" of Johnsonville, an abandoned museum mill village. Unlike more "popular" abandoned Connecticut locations, such as the state hospitals, Holy Land, or factories like Remington Arms in Bridgeport, Johnsonville is less publicized. I discovered Johnsonville for the first time myself a few years back. I was going for a drive on the back roads of Connecticut and spotted a covered bridge. My traveling companion was excited to spot the bridge and asked if we could investigate more closely. Driving

A building in the abandoned village of Johnsonville, an authentic mill town that turned into a living history museum and today sits vacant.

down the road a bit, we next came to a small white church with blue trim, with a sign out front reading "Johnsonville-Neptune Twine and Cord." At first, we did not pay it any mind, since seeing a small church in rural Connecticut is not rare. Taking a left onto Johnsonville Road, we noticed, on the right side, a cluster of buildings, fenced in with "No Trespassing" signs in front. This is when we first realized that we had stumbled onto something quite unusual. Researching the "other side" of Connecticut tourism and travel for years, I was shocked to discover such a large abandoned property without having read anything about it prior.

To me, the most striking feature of the town was the large (a few feet tall) trophy-

One of the many intriguing features of Johnsonville.

styled cup on the lawn. Driving the length of the village a few times, we saw a mill, a few houses, and what looked like a restaurant. Even though the property was definitely abandoned, it did not look as if it were in disrepair like much of abandoned Connecticut. When I got home, I asked my parents (life-long residents of Connecticut) if they had ever been to or heard about Johnsonville. They said they had not, and soon after, I took them out so that they could see it for themselves.

I decided the best place to start learning about Johnsonville was at the East Haddam Historical Society. The friendly staff introduced me to facts of the village. The 51.8-acre Johnsonville was a working mill village that began thriving in the mid-1800s and specialized in twine. The village was named after Emory Johnson, who founded the mill in the nineteenth century and who lived in the biggest house in the village. It was based around twine production in the Neptune Twine and Cord Mill, which opened in 1832. The mill, which, sadly, burned down years ago, was powered by the Moodus River. Also on site was a waterfall, a home for the mill owner, and the church. After the village stopped becoming a functioning town, Raymond Schmitt, who was wealthy from the aerospace industry, bought it in the 1960s. In addition to the buildings that were located on the property, he brought other historic buildings from that era to create a village. His intention was to create a living history museum (like a mill town version of Old Sturbridge Village or Mystic Seaport). Adding to the old houses and the church, the village also housed a restaurant called the Red House, which, along with the chapel, was used for functions, such as weddings. The area also had a sawmill, dam, schoolhouse, clock shop, toy shop, post office, blacksmith's forge, general store, and a horse barn. Schmitt even had a riverboat on the property's pond!

Johnsonville has been closed since 1994 and is available for sale. Raymond Schmitt had a run-in with the town government over land regulations and decided to close down the village. Schmitt only charged for the use of his chapel and restaurant, never an admission into the village. Some speculate he shuttered the place because his business was not doing well at the time and it was no longer in his best interest to maintain the village. A few years later, Schmitt passed away, but almost twenty years since his death, the town is still trying to sell the land as a development, but as of this writing, this endeavor has been unsuccessful. There are "No Trespassing" signs scattered along the fence of the village, but most of the village can be seen clearly from the road. The town looks empty, but not decaying. There are lights on in some of the buildings and even a Christmas tree in a window that I saw during a visit in July 2011.

Be careful though, some say that Mr. Schmitt can still be seen there today. Some day Johnsonville will be gone, so make sure to view it while you still can! Hopefully some kind of restoration or preservation will be done before it is too late.

Resort Communities
Cave Hill Resort and Sunrise Resort

Up the road from Johnsonville was — and is still to some degree — a resort community. During much of the twentieth century, camps and resorts like Cave Hill, Klar Crest, and Ted Hilton's attracted visitors who came to swim in their pools, enjoy recreational activities, and generally get away from everyday life. Once there were about forty resorts with cottage-style accommodations in the area. Today, only one remains: Cave Hill Resort. Ted Hilton's, which in its last incarnation was called Sunrise Resort and was the biggest, closed in 2008. Moodus was considered the "Catskills of Connecticut," a popular vacation destination for New Yorkers escaping summer in the city. The resorts gave vacationers luxuries such as three meals a day and classes in ballroom dancing and exercise, as well as excursions such as canoe trips on the Salmon River. On a weekend night, performers, such as Linda and the Notables, entertained on the stage of Ted Hilton's. Both Sunrise and Cave Hill were built in the first part of the twentieth century and were big draws for families. At Sunrise, facilities included paddle boats, mini-golf, a baseball field, an Olympic-sized swimming pool, and "Paradise Beach." Eventually, the state bought the park from the Johnson family, who were the owners of Sunrise Resort. The camps of Moodus could not compete with full-service luxury resorts available to today's vacationing families. For the modern family, the idea of staying in a cabin in the woods without air-conditioning, and going on nature walks, pales in comparison with an all-inclusive beachside resort vacation or a visit to an elaborate theme park.

The Sunrise Resort today adjoins the land of Machimoodus State Park, but sits abandoned and crumbling. Fallen victim to vandalism and arson, the Sunrise Resort is literally a shell of what it once was. The visitor can still see the overgrown mini-golf course, empty swimming pool, and smashed function hall. Similar to other abandoned locales, it is as if people simply disappeared from site. The latest talk was that two different developers were interested in turning the place into a water park or a Sturbridge Village-styled living history museum. Other than Cave Hill, the resorts have been demolished, abandoned, or reconfigured, such as one former resort that has been turned into My Father's House, a religious retreat center.

While at Sunrise Resort, watch out for the ghost of Ted Hilton, still said to walk the grounds.

On my visit to Machimoodus State Park, I had hoped to see the remnants of Ted Hilton's (aka Sunrise Resort) myself. After walking some trails, I met a woman who told us how to get to the resort, which abuts the Machimoodus property. Even though it is owned by the state of Connecticut, it has remained in disrepair since the purchase. There is no sign at the entrance to the resort. Since there was a chain across the entrance to the former parking lot, we parked near one of the cottages, noting signs that said, "Park closes at sunset," giving us the impression that it was "legal" to be there.

Beside the small cottages at the park's entrance was a two-story frame house with the sign "White House" above the door. A plaque with the words "I. Chapman Jr. Place 1826" was placed to the left of the front door. The exterior of this building looked to be in very good shape. We had been told that members of the Johnson family, the former owners of the property, lived on the grounds. Their neatly maintained Cape-style home was situated a small distance from the parking lot.

The parking lot, with many weed-filled cracks in the pavement, is the highest point of the resort. As we walked down the hill, to our left was an overgrown miniature golf course and a volleyball net. I talked to a visitor who had memories of coming to Ted Hilton's on his high school class trip and playing at a golf course consisting of a few holes on the grounds. We continued on to the main administrative building and dining hall, a U-shaped building. Another visitor recalled being a chaperone for a Norwich Free Academy field trip that began with a lavish breakfast buffet served in that area. Now it was filled with leaves and dirt (hopefully those were not served in the buffet). Near a wall were three vinyl cushions, creating a makeshift bed, with a half bottle of Coca Cola nearby. There were several picture windows through which we saw the dining hall, with a counter and many chairs and tables set up, almost as if they were ready for the next group's visit. Two of the windows were smashed, with broken glass on the outside concrete floor. As we turned to leave this area, we heard a thumping sound and caught a peripheral image of something fluttering. The thump seemed to come from the intact window, perhaps a bird caught inside. One side of that window was covered by a sign that said "Reserved for Laura Johnson." Exactly what was reserved for Laura Johnson was not obvious.

Near the dining building was a huge swimming pool. On this sunny day, the blue painted floor of the pool seemed iridescent, the whole thing strangely devoid of debris. This was particularly odd since Hurricane Irene had wreaked havoc in the area just a few weeks earlier.

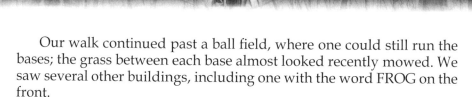
Our walk continued past a ball field, where one could still run the bases; the grass between each base almost looked recently mowed. We saw several other buildings, including one with the word FROG on the front.

We climbed the hill back to the parking lot and got a closer look at some of the cottages. One cottage had a screened back porch, its door open. I peeked in and saw a thin mattress on the hallway floor and a chair next to the mattress.

As we were ready to leave, we noticed a large sign on the lawn near a cottage. It said, "Day Guests Welcome! 1 or 2 meals and use of the grounds. July and August!" Images of Ted Hilton's (aka Sunrise Resort) in the 1950s, with people swimming in the state-of-the-art pool, sunbathing, playing tennis, enjoying top performers in the nightclub, seemed to freeze this vacationland in time. Yet, at the bottom of the sign was a telephone number and then modern technology intruded with the words, "www.sunriseresort.com." I guess the fun times were not that long ago.

Moodus Noises

Heading toward Cave Hill Resort, do not be surprised if you hear rumblings under the ground. Moodus gained notoriety for its "noises," which were first officially recorded in 1568, but heard for decades earlier by local Native Americans and early settlers who thought malevolent spirits were causing a ruckus. In reality, the Moodus Noises were and still are tiny earthquakes. The location of the Moodus Noises comes from the proximity of Mt. Tom. Native American legend interpreted the noises to be the doing of Hobomoko, a god who would send his thunder, either in loud, brutal blasts or in softer, calmer tones, depending on his mood. The area, still called Moodus today, is a shortened version of "Machimoodus," which meant in the local dialect "place of bad noises." The Machimoodus, who were a sub-group of the larger Wangunk tribe, were located here. Other surrounding Native American tribes thought that the Machimoodus tribe was able to directly understand the rumblings of Hobomoko. The Machimoodus would try to appease the angry god through prayer and sacrifice and based their religion around the noises. (Heck, without the knowledge of modern science, it would be a good idea to say some prayers to stop the earth from shaking all around without notice!)

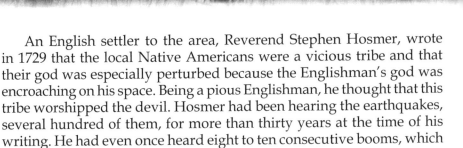

An English settler to the area, Reverend Stephen Hosmer, wrote in 1729 that the local Native Americans were a vicious tribe and that their god was especially perturbed because the Englishman's god was encroaching on his space. Being a pious Englishman, he thought that this tribe worshipped the devil. Hosmer had been hearing the earthquakes, several hundred of them, for more than thirty years at the time of his writing. He had even once heard eight to ten consecutive booms, which he likened to small explosions, canon shots, or thunder.

There were many other explanations as to the cause of the earth-shaking sounds. One popular theory was that the black witches of Haddam were battling the white witches of Moodus, like a modern day football rivalry. The battle that took place in the caves below Mt. Tom were illuminated by a glowing gemstone. Included in this version was a supreme being referred to as King Machimoddi who would tell them to knock it off after a while by using his wand. When he ceased the witch-fight, the use of his wand would cause the thundering sound, as the witches flew high into the sky. Another theory involved a wizard named Dr. Steel, a mysterious man who lived on Mt. Tom. He would try with all his might to figure out the root of the noises. One night, while digging through the mountain's caves, he found the gemstone, after which the noises ceased. Soon after though, Steel took a boat to England, but never reached his destination, as the boat sank, with Steel and the stone on it. When the rumblings started happening once again, the Native Americans believed that a new stone was growing in the caves of Mt. Tom.

The legendary explanations of the Moodus Noises, from the anger of an evil deity to a witch battle, have been handed down for centuries. Along with the legends have been scientific explanations. In 1761, the biggest earthquake in the area occurred, which was felt all the way to New York and Boston. The destruction of chimneys was the extent of the reported damage. In October of 1888, the *Hartford Times* reported that the Moodus Noises were back, shaking houses after a cessation of twelve years. That article contained no reference to an angry Hobomoko, however. In the last thirty or so years, the Moodus Noises have continued, so much so that the Boston College Observatory in Weston, Massachusetts, takes readings via seismographs located in Moodus. In 1982, there were hundreds of these "noises," now termed "mini-quakes." The biggest quake, occurring in 1982, hit 2.9 on the Richter scale, which is not house-shattering, but could definitely be disconcerting to those nearby who do not know of the area's history. During a span of about a month in 1987, 175 mini-quakes erupted, some of them sounding like a gunshot, thunder, or canon fire, much the same way they were described by Reverend Hosmer 250 years earlier. Even more recently, in March, 2011, a mini-quake with the magnitude of 1.3 vibrated the walls of nearby houses in the Moodus Reservoir section of town. Although scientists are able to determine that these quakes are natural and not the work of Hobomoko, King Machimoddi, or Dr. Steel, they still have questions.

It's interesting that a tiny section of a small town in rural Connecticut is home to a vast array of sights and sounds. The ruins of Moodus's former glory can be seen in the once touristy spot of Johnsonville, which families visited when they stayed at resorts like Sunrise and Klar Crest, neither of which exists today. Could it be Hobomoko cursing the visitors to the area or is it just coincidence that they deteriorated?

Moodus is located near the intersection of Routes 151 and 149 in East Haddam.

2.
Holy Land USA
Location: Waterbury

One of Connecticut's strangest sites is "Holy Land USA" in Waterbury. Holy Land was created in the 1950s by John Greco, a pious Catholic and a lawyer. He claimed to have heard a call from God and, to show his devotion, built a mini Jerusalem out of random material, including aluminum, concrete, and household junk. In his miniature city are a mini sphinx, "Herrod's Place," and the mysterious catacombs.

The crumbling hillside of Holy Land's Little Bethlehem.

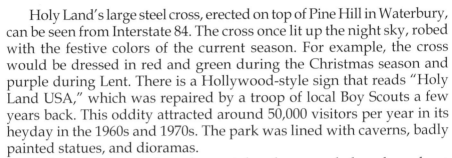

Holy Land's large steel cross, erected on top of Pine Hill in Waterbury, can be seen from Interstate 84. The cross once lit up the night sky, robed with the festive colors of the current season. For example, the cross would be dressed in red and green during the Christmas season and purple during Lent. There is a Hollywood-style sign that reads "Holy Land USA," which was repaired by a troop of local Boy Scouts a few years back. This oddity attracted around 50,000 visitors per year in its heyday in the 1960s and 1970s. The park was lined with caverns, badly painted statues, and dioramas.

Today, the statues have been stolen, have eroded, or have been decapitated, except for a pedestal with a statue of Jesus at the top. Behind every turn and overgrown bush lies another mind-boggling testament to Greco's strange religious fervor. An enormous concrete wall displays words defending the sacrament of marriage, and three crosses depicting Calvary loom above the unsuspecting visitor. The crudeness of the design of Holy Land is the most striking feature of the park. The hodgepodge of materials used to create it resembles the creativity of a child.

There seems to be no real rhyme or reason to the layout of the park. Holy Land is built on a rising hillside. At the entrance to the park, one sees a life-size Jesus statue. Two main paths snake on either side of the bulk of the park, winding up the hillside. Scattered between the two uphill walkways are unprofessionally made models of biblical scenes or places, including the Last Supper, Christ's tomb, and Herrod's Place. All of these are crumbling down, nearing a state of total demolition. Near the top of the hill is the model of Calvary. The most well known feature of the park is the steel cross, located at the very top where all the paths converge.

Holy Land USA has steadily declined since Greco's death in 1986. Abandoned on the top of Slocum Road, in Waterbury, the park remains under the ownership of a group of nuns from Bristol, Connecticut. These nuns do not look kindly on visitors, since most people visit for the wrong reasons. It would be wonderful to go back in time and be able to experience the mini-pyramid, the "Plague of Popes," and the "Every Day is Christmas" exhibits in all their glory.

Like many tourist attractions, Holy Land once had a gift shop, and a large number of parking spots. The park has been officially closed since 1984, but remains today, although smaller each day, as both vandals and Mother Nature do their part to make Holy Land USA part of the past.

Holy Land matches the unlikely duo of roadside attraction and religious piety. To many this may be seen as tacky or even sacrilegious, while others view it as a true place of devotion.

3.
Gungywamp
Location: Groton

"Gungywamp," a word associated with local Algonquin Native people, means "land of swamp," although some say it comes from the Gaelic word meaning "Church of the People." Groton, Connecticut, is the location of Gungywamp, and Salem, a few towns away, has a Gungy Road, whose name obviously derives from the same source. The reputation of Gungywamp, a series of stone chambers, grows by the year. Some experts say that these formations, including a calendar rock configuration and other strangely placed boulders, is proof of a pre-Columbian Society in New England, possibly that of the Ancient Celts. Others argue that this intriguingly unusual outpost of rock formations is only a colonial era sheep farm. Whatever the case may be, the former YMCA camp land close to the Naval Base in Groton certainly has an allure to it. During the fall of 2011, I was graciously led on a most comprehensive tour of this area.

Some archeologists hypothesize that St. Brendan, the famed Irish voyager, while en-route to find Paradise, actually landed in America, more specifically, in present day Groton (and if Groton is not paradise, I don't know what is!). This school of thought ascertains that the Gungywamp Archeological Site's origin is early Irish Christian. Proof includes a stone chamber into which the sun shines directly only at the autumnal and vernal equinoxes. The vernal equinox relates to the Christian holiday of Easter. Small light openings like this were found in small, rural churches of Ireland erected around this same time. Also present at Gungywamp are Chi-Rho symbols, which are the first two letters of the word Christos or Christ. As well, charcoal present in a fire pit has been dated back to the 500s, although there is no proof whose charcoal it was. Alas, no Celtic writing (Ogham) was found on site, either.

Although some archeologists support the notion of St. Brendan as the key to the mystery of Gungywamp, others see ancient Celts or Norsemen as logical answers to the question of Gungywamp's origin. Professor and Gungywamp Society member William Dopirak believes otherwise. Mr. Dopirak led our small group on a private tour of Gungywamp. We approached Gungywamp by parking near a rusted gate that led to the former driveway of the YMCA camp that was closed

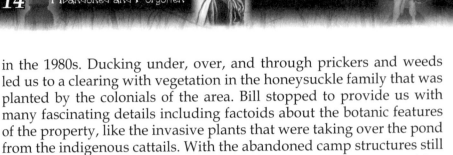

in the 1980s. Ducking under, over, and through prickers and weeds led us to a clearing with vegetation in the honeysuckle family that was planted by the colonials of the area. Bill stopped to provide us with many fascinating details including factoids about the botanic features of the property, like the invasive plants that were taking over the pond from the indigenous cattails. With the abandoned camp structures still standing, or more appropriately, leaning, an interesting juxtaposition was created between the forlorn structures and the natural vegetation, as well as the glacial outpouring. In walking closer to the Gungywamp site, Bill showed us the only proof of "real" Celtics to the area, as he pointed to a decrepit basketball court.

Luckily, our visit was on a crisp New England autumn day, perfect windbreaker weather. Leaves were hanging on the trees by a thread, wild turkeys were gobbling out of our view, and the bright blue sky was dotted with white puffy clouds. We soon veered away from the campsite and walked over a makeshift log bridge as if it were a balance beam to guard us from the pond runoff below. (Of course, my foot slipped directly into the bog.) As we trudged through swamp and muck, eventually reaching the base of the steep hill that would take us to Gungywamp, Bill pointed out that there was also evidence that the area nearby once included a cranberry bog.

As we continued on our hike, Bill noted prime examples of glacial striae that occurred by rocks rubbing against each other from movement by the glacier. He told us that the ice once covering the very ground we were walking upon had a height of half a mile and extended all the way to the southern side of Long Island. He added that Long Island Sound was at this time a freshwater lake. Even more confounding was Bill's statement that this area of Connecticut was once landlocked to the northwestern part of Africa during the time of Pangea, which led to similar landscapes in the two regions.

On the way to Gungywamp, the first structure that we were introduced to was the Echo Chamber. Looking at this formation from a specific angle distinctly shows the visage of a Native American. It was a bit jarring to see the word "PARTY" spray-painted in huge letters on the rock.

The sites of Gungywamp are labeled with small signs designating them as "Site 1," "Site 2," and so on. Some say that Site 2 was an ice house, while others, more sensationally, call this the tomb chamber. Another possibility was that this was a birthing chamber. When Bill first mentioned the term "birthing chamber," I did not know quite what to think of it, but then he clued me into his personal theory of a possible use for Gungywamp as a colonial sheep farm. So the birthing chamber refers to an area for sheep to give birth, not humans. Phew!

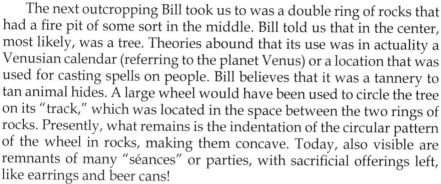

The next outcropping Bill took us to was a double ring of rocks that had a fire pit of some sort in the middle. Bill told us that in the center, most likely, was a tree. Theories abound that its use was in actuality a Venusian calendar (referring to the planet Venus) or a location that was used for casting spells on people. Bill believes that it was a tannery to tan animal hides. A large wheel would have been used to circle the tree on its "track," which was located in the space between the two rings of rocks. Presently, what remains is the indentation of the circular pattern of the wheel in rocks, making them concave. Today, also visible are remnants of many "séances" or parties, with sacrificial offerings left, like earrings and beer cans!

The Calendar Chamber is the most talked about feature of Gungywamp. It is a stone cellar that has a large entrance on one side and a small opening on the opposite. During the weeks of the vernal and autumnal equinoxes, the sun sets due west and light shines through this chamber. Actually, what rises and sets due east and west is Orion's Belt. To some, this chamber is evidence of ancient Celts in the area, but to others the light shaft that signifies the equinox directly represents the planting and harvesting times for a calendar-less colonial society. The chamber itself has a small opening on the right-hand wall that can be easy to overlook. When crawled through, the secret area is so tall that it can fit an adult standing, albeit bent over. This spot could have been used to stash armaments or to provide a place of refuge.

Site 6, which Bill believes to be a type of warehouse, could have been used to store hides, sometimes dyeing them with berries. It was also a possibility that Gungywamp could have been only used seasonally as a hunting lodge. Site 7 included a fireplace and a kitchen, and Bill speculated that this was the primary residence. Further evidence of the area being a colonial sheep farm includes the height of the stone walls. These stone walls wind their way through the property, up the hillsides and down the valleys, constructed in straight patterns. They were, however, not large enough to fence cattle in, but were a perfect size to pen sheep. In his discussion of these stone walls, Bill added that during the 1800s, at the height of stonewall popularity in New England, stonewalls placed contiguously could wrap the earth many times over.

Continuing down the path, we came to another sheep birthing chamber that had since collapsed and at the time of my visit; Hurricane Irene had left its mark with a fallen tree lying across. A similar structure can be seen off of Fire Street in nearby Montville. Site 3 is also a birthing chamber, including drainage for waste, and would have had a wooden top on it. In the days before modern routes like 12 and 1, the path that we were walking on was used as a major buggy thoroughfare. Walking further into Gungywamp, we noticed stones standing in a strange, but seemingly purposeful way. About a dozen flat stones standing upright in almost an equidistant length apart has given Bill some ideas for their use. He surmises that the standing stones, which resemble an eagle's head, were used as a bracing wall, a place to shear sheep, or somewhere to sell grain in enticement of the passing drivers. At Site 9 a second row of standing stones can be found.

Site 10 is across from the standing stones and is called a "cursing stone," based on a Celtic legend. The cursing stone is a rock resembling a small table (altar) that is embedded as part of the stone wall. Today, small stones are put on top of the large, flat, table-like altar. A small stone was put on the altar when a curse was placed on a victim. The cursing stone is located on the right side of the carriage road and directly across from a sloping hill. Bill hypothesized that the "cursing stone" was actually a drainage pipe. In order for rain to run off from the hillside and not pool up on the path, a gap below the cursing stone was dug. The table rock would act like a sluiceway. The small rocks on the table top would be used as weapons to attack caribou or deer stampeding through the bog, which was located to the right of the path, and was the destination of the runoff. So whether the rock was used as an altar or a primitive form of drainage, the story of the "cursing stone" is just another unique facet in the annals of Gungywamp lore.

Standing stones at Gungywamp, which are theorized to have been used as a bracing wall, holding pens for sheep shearing, or compartments for grain selling.

The last site that we were shown on our tour was a speculated location of a barn or carriage house. This one was rebuilt by the Gungywamp Society. A skull from the 1800s was found near this site, and the bones are still there, hidden from view. The skull is on exhibit at Nick Bellantoni's Archaeoloy Museum exhibit at UCONN. (The museum is included in another chapter.)

The Gungywamp Society controls most of the land in the Gungywamp property. Gungywamp's furthest inland sites are located on private property. This includes the far portion of the pond and the

A carriage house or barn at Gungywamp that the Gungywamp Society rebuilt.

"Cliff of Tears," which legend says makes the visitor suddenly feel sad. Grown men and women have both fallen victim to the moroseness of the Cliff. This was the site of an old quarry. Sadly, or should I say happily, since today, this location is off limits to the public. At least today's visitors will not leave Gungywamp feeling upset!

Whether Gungywamp is the last remnant of a colonial sheep farm or a destination on St. Brendan's voyage, it surely is a place full of intrigue. The rock formations alone make it worthy of a visit. Insight into the geological history of the area brings it further to life. If you would like to find out more about the Gungywamp Society, please visit www. gungywamp.com; although the society has since folded, its website gives information on visiting. Gungywamp is comprised of beautiful wooded acreage, a welcome respite from the chaos of daily life. It is a perfect place to take a woodland walk. As you are visiting, picture the place's vivid and storied past. Whom do you think settled here?

Gungywamp is located on Gungywamp Road in Groton. Although there are "No Parking" signs along the left-hand side of the road (heading east), the access trails are found in the inlets of the road. Many thanks to Professor Bill Dopirak for taking the better part of an afternoon to show and teach my readers about the many mysteries of Gungywamp.

4.
Roxbury's Mine Hill
Location: Roxbury

Mine Hill in Roxbury stands today as a testament to nineteenth century American industrialism and ingenuity, and conversely, to the powerful force of nature. You may ask, how can such a locale be indicative of two very different sides of a coin. Currently, the space known as Mine Hill is overflowing with natural beauty. Four miles of trails let hikers and nature lovers enjoy the vistas of this section of western Connecticut, close to the banks of the Shepaug River. This protected land is abundant with wildlife and provides a serene retreat for the day hiker, although picturesque and natural were adjectives not always used to describe Mine Hill. Any visitor to the reservation can attest to its industrial heritage by looking at the restored blast furnace that still adorns the grounds.

In an area of town previously known as Spruce Hill, this rock-strewn land was too difficult to reap for even the most stubborn Yankee farmers. Eventually, industry paved its own path through the hills along the Shepaug. During a small span of years in the mid 1800s, Mine Hill was a major steel and iron manufacturer. Even more lucrative was the granite and other kinds of rock that were quarried from the area. A small, thriving community sprung up around the mines, called Chalybes. Today, the only remnant of the past village is a road with its namesake. Once upon a time, this now ghost town employed 200 migrant workers, and included a general store, grist mill, and creamery. During its heyday, Mine Hill produced ten tons of pig iron per day! What is now again heavily wooded forest was cut down to provide fuel for the mines. Mine Hill's blast furnace only ran for five years, between 1867 and 1872. Its rapid decline was in part due to outdated and ill-working materials, as well as a lack of easy transportation (train transport finally arrived, albeit too late for the iron production, in 1871). Before the advent of the train, cart and animal transport was in use.

Colonists first searched this area for silver in 1765. In the next hundred years, industry began slowly but steadily, building two furnaces with a complex in fruition by 1865. The complex included underground tunnels, a blast furnace, paths for donkey transport, roasting ovens, and a rolling mill. The mine workers used only hand tools and blast powder to further their excavation and had to work by candlelight!

Even though iron production did not flourish for long in Roxbury, the granite from its quarries was used to build impressive structures, including Grand Central Station and the 59th Street Bridge in New York City, as well as the town library in Roxbury. In 1978, the Roxbury Land Trust bought the Mine Hill area and a year later, it was added to the National Register of Historic Places. In total there were eight granite quarries at Mine Hill. There are still three main tunnels that are located in there, attached by vertical mineshafts. The mines are off limits to the public due to the danger of their nature, but they are an important bat habitat. Also located at the preserve are large holes, most likely used in the mining process, which are juxtaposed with the park's natural bubbling brooks.

The blast furnace still stands today, as well. It is made of the Roxbury granite, quarried nearby. The true immensity of the furnace is astounding, even though its tall chimney no longer stands. To use the blast furnace, rocks and substances like charcoal, limestone, and marble were poured into the top chimney of the furnace. The fire inside the chimney reached temperatures up to 3,000 degrees Fahrenheit. The substances were then heated to make 100-pound iron bars, known as pig iron. Why pig iron? When the hot iron was put into molds, the blocks of iron together in the molds resembled little piglets nursing from a large mama pig.

The mining process itself was quite an endeavor, as well. Ore was mined in the granite rock and then loaded into carts. The carts ran on narrow gauge rail tracks. (Just like in cartoons!). The ore was then cooked in ovens and refined in order to separate the iron from the stone.

Today, Mine Hill is preserved as a park, both for its natural beauty and industrial heritage. Nature, which once was leveled to be used as fuel in the mining process, once again has overtaken the land.

Mine Hill Park is located on Mine Hill Road in Roxbury, close to CT Route 67.

5.
Daniel's Village
A Tale of Colonial Killingly
Location: Killingly

Located on a back road in bucolic Northeastern Connecticut lies the village, or what is left of it, called Daniel's Village. The remnants of this once-thriving mill community dot a section of the Five Mile River on the Killingly–Putnam border. The community that was home to one of the first textile mills in America now only contains evidence of its former self and it has become one of Connecticut's ghost towns.

Daniel's Village, which was originally called Talbot's Mills, was first settled by a man named John Parks in the 1720s. In 1725, the first grist mill was built along with a homestead. By the mid to late 1700s, other settlers built more homes, a tanyard, a schoolhouse, and another mill. In 1814, the town was home to one of the original textile mills in America. In 1845, the property was bought by Taylor Daniels and renamed Daniel's Village. Working life in Daniel's Village was similar to that of many of New England's industrial towns. The mill employed men, women, and children with shifts as long as 12-14 hours with an unbalanced pay scale where men earned a higher hourly wage than women and children. A fire in 1861 that obliterated the textile mill led to the rapid decline of the mill village. The 1960s brought a yoga retreat to the banks of the Five Mile River in the former Daniel's Village location. Eastern Connecticut at that time was not a hotbed of New Age thinking and eastern religion, and the yoga center soon after moved to Virginia. In 1976, Daniel's Village was placed on the National Register of Historic Places as an archeological district. Albert F. Bartovics, from Brown University, wrote a lengthy thesis on his archeological discoveries at Daniel's Village. It was published in 1981).

During the factory's heyday, the mill was called the Killingly Manufacturing Company. At one time, Killingly was the greatest cotton manufacturing town in Connecticut, and the mill at Daniel's Village spearheaded this trend. Killingly is a town comprised of many mill villages, including Ballouville, Attawaugan, and Danielson where the factories still stand. Today, what is left of Daniel's Village lies just south of the Putnam border; but at the time of its creation, Putnam, along with Thompson, were included in the municipality of Killingly. Just up the river, this area of Killingly was also home to the Chestnut Hill Purchase, which was another early incorporated section of town. Included here was Killingly's first town pound dating from the 1730s, an old tavern from the 1740s, and a town common.

Daniel's Village is located on the banks of the Five Mile River at the intersection of Stone and River roads in the town of Killingly. Today, the visitor will find only a few remaining clues to the community that once thrived on the side of the river. One dwelling remains, called the Stone House, which was the mill owner's house, and hence the name; it is made of stone. Currently, this is a private home, so please do not trespass. The stone is unusual since most colonial houses in New England were made of wood, with stone being used in the creation of stone walls. This building material is more typically found in other states, such as Pennsylvania. The waterfall, embedded in stone, also remains as a reminder of the power source of the mill that once stood nearby.

Across from the Stone House, foundations remain from buildings toppled long ago. In this same area, one can also see the Tunnel House. At first glance from the street, this unusual building easily goes unnoticed, but with further inspection, one can see an earthen mound rising from the ground. With a closer look, the visitor will discover that this mound is actually a tunnel that protrudes a few feet above the ground. Even deeper investigation will lead to the realization that the front of this tunnel is an abandoned converted "tunnel house" of sorts. The front of the house overhangs a stagnant, algae-ridden sluiceway that once carried water to other parts of the village. A peek into the front of the house shows how the functional passageway was turned into a unique living space. Nearby, the visitor can see foundations and entrances into the tunnel house equipped with living necessities like a kitchen sink, staircases, and light bulbs.

The Five Mile River waterfall powered the early settlement of Daniel's Village.

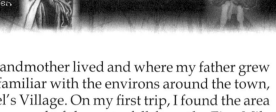

Killingly is where my grandmother lived and where my father grew up. Even though he is very familiar with the environs around the town, he had never heard of Daniel's Village. On my first trip, I found the area peaceful, but eerie. Only the sound of the waterfall from the Five Mile River and crickets permeated the air. To the passerby, the village would go unnoticed because the Stone House is all that remains. The solitude of the house, the foundations, and the tunnel dwelling together add a bit more mystery to this abandoned village.

While You're There:

Logee's Greenhouses

The huge selection will impress even the most blasé horticulturist and provide an afternoon activity for the armchair botanist with a stroll through the vast greenhouses. Logee's started in 1892. A lemon tree was planted in 1900 into the ground of one of the greenhouses, and it is still growing and producing five-pound lemons. While I was there, I saw lots of them! Logee's is known worldwide for its begonias. The neat part about visiting the greenhouses is that they are wild, not precisely sculpted and manicured like many similar places. As you walk down the narrow passageways, be careful because you are often attacked by branches of trees and plants. Their catalog is professionally photographed and allows even the West Coast plant aficionado to order from their exquisite selection. The plants are shipped in 2.5- or 4-inch pots. Visiting Logee's is less like visiting a greenhouse and more like visiting a museum. A trip to the greenhouses will surely yield a purchase of some sorts. Heck, you never know when you will need a lemon tree for your living room!

Check out Logee's Greenhouses at 141 North Street in Danielson for an exotic array of flowers and plants.

6.
The Norwich State Hospital
Norwich and Preston

Abandoned institutional, municipal, and civic buildings have become America's ruins. Once standing proudly as testaments of modernity and forward thinking, today they remain as forays into America's architectural and bureaucratic past. Although a few still stand tall today, most are leaning, demolished, or converted into other uses. After the "modern" building designs of the '50s, '60s, and '70s, the architecture of these buildings seems ancient, but not long ago they were displays of a progressive society. Why today, when these empty buildings are literal shells of their former selves, are we drawn to them? Is it the discovery of the past lying inside the present? Is it the fact that they stand in their current state only for a fleeting moment, for soon they will be either torn down or redeveloped? Is it the curiosity they invoke in us, conjuring up images of the unknown?

The Kirkbride Building of the Norwich State Hospital crumbles from years of disuse.

The abandoned mental institution is a prime example of the intrigue of the unknown. Straightjackets, lobotomies, and morgues—these are gruesome images that are commonly associated with such buildings. In reality, even though all these were relevant and were part of institutional life, they were not nearly as ever-present as one might think. From the outside, mental hospitals were once

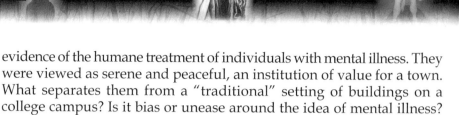

evidence of the humane treatment of individuals with mental illness. They were viewed as serene and peaceful, an institution of value for a town. What separates them from a "traditional" setting of buildings on a college campus? Is it bias or unease around the idea of mental illness? Is it the tales, thoughts, and legends that surround such places? Is it the decaying state that many of these grandiose buildings have fallen into?

Compare, for instance, two sister institutions, Fairfield Hills State Hospital in Newtown and Norwich State Hospital in Preston and Norwich. Both were built in the first decades of the twentieth century, and both were closed down by Governor Rowland after years of continued deinstitutionalization. During my first trip to Fairfield Hills, I was greeted by dog walkers and workers on lunch break, enjoying the beautiful day to stroll around and get fresh air. The lawns were nicely mowed with active sports fields flanking the hospital property. The buildings were vacant, but not crumbling. They were empty, except for a town office that was located in one of the former hospital structures. Although I had heard strange rumors of the place at the time and had known about its history, as well as its use in television shows and movies, there was not a foreboding atmosphere; on the contrary, it was cheery, upbeat. Although most of the institution was inactive, the town preserved the hospital grounds and presented it as a friendly place to take a walk.

Contrast this with Norwich. The grounds are off-limits to everyone. It is patrolled by a security force in white pickup trucks as the buildings are left to rot and wait for the wrecking ball (which started early in 2011). The lawns are not maintained, the grounds are littered with "No Trespassing" signs, and overall, the place feels unwelcome. Yes, the Norwich State Hospital has had its share of inhumanity and patient neglect, but the decaying buildings and unmaintained grounds have contributed to its notoriety, causing this place to lurk in people's minds.

Let's go back in time to 1904. Imagine Brewster's Neck (the location of the hospital) before the thirty-six-story skyscraper housing the Mohegan Sun Casino loomed across the Thames River, before the Gold Star Highway connected the area to Route 395, before Routes 2 and 2A became major thoroughfares linking casino to casino. The Norwich Hospital for the Insane, later to be known as the Norwich State Hospital, was recently opened to much fanfare. The mental hospital was looked at as a progressive institution for the betterment of the "insane" or the "feeble minded." Dr. Henry M. Pollock, who was the first superintendent, had liberal ideas concerning care for mental patients. He championed innovative programs, like the patient-tended farm thath supplied food for the hospital's kitchen.

Mental hospitals tended to follow two main architectural plans, known as the Cottage Plan and the Kirkbride Plan. In the Kirkbride Plan, the buildings took on a castle or fortress-like shape, with an administration building as a center piece with flanking sides to the left and to the right. Danvers State Hospital in Massachusetts was a prime example of this style. The other popular style, the Cottage Plan, is also capped by an architecturally impressive administration building, but the adjacent buildings are not attached, and instead, are spread out on the grounds in full symmetry, but not connected. The Norwich Hospital was an example of this hospital plan until the later building campaigns unbalanced the symmetrical layout.

The first two buildings on the hospital property were Awl and Salmon. Each of these buildings held over 100 patients and was divided into eight wards, with sitting rooms, bathrooms, and dining rooms. The patients were separated first by gender and then by condition. The goal of the interior design of the buildings was to create a sterile feeling, which would be sustained for many years. Over the next twenty years, many buildings were added. The hospital flourished under its first superintendents, but by the early thirties, the state was not giving the hospital the proper funds to maintain such a vast facility. The institution, throughout the thirties, steadily declined, and by the last years, was not adequate. In addition, some of the staff mistreated the patients. Many of the descriptions of patient life during this period reveal it to be the worst in the history of the hospital, which is tragic because for much of the hospital's use as an institution, it was state-of-the-art and had a reputation of being a relatively good place to live.

The Awl Building, for most of its existence, housed the most "well behaved" female patients. The building had fancy parlors and the patients had many privileges, such as going downtown by way of the trolley that was extended from downtown Norwich to the hospital in the early part of the twentieth century, or the ability to roam the grounds, at a time when much of society was not ready for this. In contrast, the Salmon building has always been somewhat of a controversy at Norwich. After its initial use as an all-male ward, it was implemented as a maximum security facility for the criminally insane. The building was filled with cages upon cages for the patients, often with two or more patients placed in one cage. Legend has it that if two criminally insane patients were put in such close quarters, at least one of them would wind up dead before long. If patients were acting up, they were locked out on the day porches on the backside of the building.

Brigham and Bell were the most impressive looking buildings on campus. They rose three stories from the ground, and contained an attic and a basement. They were built in the French Gothic style, and on the back, are two wings of green screened-in porches, with fifteen panels of porch per floor. They are painted institutional green. Bell (for female) and Brigham (male), both built around 1908, housed patients with ground privileges. Some patients though, if acting out of line, were punished by being confined on the porches outside, even in the winter. On Sundays, in better weather, the hospital was opened to the public for tours. The orderlies sometimes put the patients on the porches to be gawked at by the visitors. Staff resided in the attics of these buildings, often cohabiting with bats. Since deinstitutionalization was occurring as early as the '60s, the numbers of patients in the hospital dropped and buildings were closed. Bell was closed in 1968. Today, Bell's rooms are cluttered with chairs, wheelchairs, surgical devices, and other medical items. The green screens are falling apart, creating blackened gaps that resemble open-mouthed smiles on these ominous buildings.

The next series of buildings were all built around 1908, and these included White and Cutter, the male and female semi-violent dorms, and the violent dorms, Dix and Stribling. Dix and Stribling had large glassed-in porches on their back side. Horrible stories are told of these dorms, including patients being sent to a room with only a drain, or the orderlies making the patients sit in a tiny corral of chairs, which they were not permitted to leave, even to use the bathroom. If they had to go to the bathroom, doing so in their clothes was the only option. If they tore at their soiled clothing, they were sent to the second floor, which had even worse conditions. Once their clothing was ripped, they did not receive new ones, so nearly naked patients ran about; some were tied to benches and others secluded in little rooms.

When Superintendent Bryan came to the hospital in the early 1940s, the hospital was in disarray, due to inadequate state funding and the effects of the Great Depression. These problems were compounded by the prevailing attitude that mental patients did not need pleasant or exceptionally clean facilities. When Bryan arrived, he had the buildings, especially the ones in the poorest condition, renovated; he encouraged the decoration of the interiors, such as putting curtains up and creating other home-like touches. Today, these buildings exude a forbidding aura, but in reality, much of the time that they were functioning, they were brimming with pride and concern for patients, and were most certainly not prison-like.

By this time period, the hospital had the workings of a self-contained community. The buildings and grounds resembled a lovely college campus, with its three-storied French Gothic administration building, adorned with gables and spires. The Norwich Hospital had its own fire department, general hospital (for patients and staff), hair salons, and bowling alleys. Like any other town, it had a greenhouse, a morgue, a few theaters, ball fields, a pond, a roller skating rink, and a scientific research center. Unlike most towns, however, the research center conducted experiments on monkeys to attempt to create new treatments for mental patients. In addition to the multiple facilities above ground, there was a unique tunnel system. Underground tunnels connect almost every building on the campus to one another. One of their initial uses was the transportation of patients. Later though, they were used solely for pipes, but also could serve as a fallout shelter in Cold War Connecticut.

The last building campaign began in 1952, with the new laundry building and state-of-the-art powerhouse. These last buildings either had one function like a laboratory, or were massive modern structures with many functions, such as housing, treatment rooms, salons, auditoriums, dining halls, and so on. The year 1955 saw the opening of the Russell Building, its sole purpose was Occupational Therapy. When it was built, it was recognized as state-of-the art with large windows, where the sunlight was thought to be therapeutic to the patients. It was the first of its kind in Connecticut. Attitudes of the general public started to change toward the mentally ill during this time period.

Along with the practice of occupational therapy, another progressive practice was giving the patients vocational responsibilities to help them with their rehabilitation, instead of being kept inside in a cage-like room. One city dweller, when witnessing a patient working, proclaimed, "you can't tell *them* from people," in part showing that eyes were finally being opened up, that individuals with mental illness were no different from "normal" people.

By the final building campaign at the hospital (1950s-'60s), most patients were admitted to the hospital for 30-60 days, instead of being there for their lifetime. The Lodge Building, which took the place of three buildings that had housed female patients, had many services within its walls. Included in this building were a beauty parlor, an occupational therapy room, a central lobby, an auditorium, three dining rooms, a nurses' station, six wards, electro and hydro therapy rooms, and a chapel.

The biggest of all the hospital buildings was built in 1960, named after a former doctor, Ronald Kettle. The Kettle Building replaced many of the smaller more antiquated ones. New medical methods were practiced here and in the Research Center, including lobotomies and hydrotherapy, both new techniques in dealing with mental illness. At this time, Norwich was considered one of two lobotomy capitals of Connecticut, following a trend moving across the United States. The hospital became a lobotomy factory. About 750 lobotomies were performed by Dr. William B. Scoville and Dr. Benjamin B. Whitcomb, working in both Norwich and Middletown. By the mid-1960s, lobotomies were replaced by drug therapy and electro-shock, both of which were administered at Norwich Hospital.

By the 1970s deinstitutionalization took over and the number of buildings in active use at the Norwich Hospital diminished greatly.

Since the hospital shut its last doors in 1996, it has grown a reputation, not only based on fact, but also on legend. The stigma of institutionalization increased as the years passed, and the hospital fell into further disarray. By the time hospital was discontinued by the state of Connecticut in the '90s, some of the buildings on the property had not been used, or fully used, for thirty years.

As a teenager and being personally intrigued by this massive property, I was interested in finding out what went on there. Instead of hearing stories of the progressive treatment of patients or in truth what a hospital of this capacity was used for, I heard gruesome anecdotes — tales of what "really" went on there...stories of patients waving bed sheets out the window with "Help Me" written on them, others committing suicide by jumping to their deaths. The burgeoning teenage populace of New London County grew up in the shadow of these vacant shells and became intrigued by this set of numerous buildings that seemed to have been abandoned "forever." And then, thanks to the Internet and its presence on TV shows *Ghost Hunters* and *Celebrity Paranormal Project* (where Tony Little "you can do it!" hunted for ghosts), Norwich State's infamy exploded.

What makes this place legendary? Is it the state of disrepair coupled with presumption of what mental illness is and the assumed maltreatment of the patients? For whatever the reason, even in today's modern society, the Norwich State Hospital retains its ghostly associations. One Norwich resident spoke of a time when he witnessed a "ghost hearse" pulling away from one of the buildings, heading towards the cemetery that abuts the property. Another person spoke of a "room full of blood" in the Ribicoff Research Center. When I spoke with a guard at the abandoned hospital, he told a story of a hand brushing the top of his head as he entered a building late one night, looking for trespassers. In researching the architectural campaigns of the hospital, the eeriest encounter I had occurred was while walking through the connecting tunnels and exploring the adjacent rooms. One room was so cold I could see my breath, while all the nearby rooms had the same moderate temperature.

Norwich's sister hospital, Fairfield Hills, in Newtown, closed around the same time as Norwich and served the same function for the western part of the state. Recently, the town has begun to rehab the hospital site for other uses. The first Connecticut state hospital to open was Connecticut Valley Hospital in Middletown. This is the only state hospital in Connecticut that is still functioning, although it is only a shell of what it used to be.

Connecticut, like most states in the country, also had tuberculosis sanitoriums. Uncas on Thames in Norwich, Undercliff Sanatorium in Meriden, and Seaside Sanatorium in Waterford are all examples of these. Seaside, a picturesque building with a prominent spire, sits literally next to the sea on the beach close to Harkness State Park. It was once solely a children's center and is the work of renowned architect Cass Gilbert.

Private hospitals like Silver Hill in New Canaan and Hartford's Institute of the Living served the wealthier set. Many of these institutions are now abandoned, including Fairfield Hills, part of CVH, Seaside, and Undercliff, and have ghost stories attributed to them, as so many vacant institutional buildings do.

Just like Norwich State Hospital, much of Connecticut Valley Hospital in Middletown today lies in abandonment.

Former institutions are testaments to a certain time and theory of treatment of individuals with mental illness and in some cases physical illness. Just as the practice of institutionalization is, for the most part, an idea of the past, the magnificent buildings that once housed these practices and ideas are passing, too. Almost all have been demolished, (in better cases) refurbished, or are biding their time before they are destroyed legally or by arson. At the time of this writing, the Norwich State Hospital is being partially dismantled and will soon be only a memory of those whom it has shaped in some capacity. There is a movement to save the administration building; only time will tell if it works. This property, located on Route 12 in Preston and Norwich, is filled with "No Trespassing" signs, and those who are caught on the premises may face serious consequences. From Route 12, the passer-by can legally still witness the wonder and majesty of what lurked there... and what may still....

While You're There:

High Rollers Lounge

Check out the High Rollers Lounge at Foxwoods Resort and Casino. A bowling alley with chandeliers in every lane, tons of flat screens to watch the game on while sitting on plush couches, this is not your grandfather's bowling alley!

A polar opposite from the abandoned hospital, the casino provides "Las Vegas style" entertainment, with big name concerts and shows, slot machines, table games, and many, many choices of cuisine.

Foxwoods is located close to the hospital property in Ledyard on Route 2.

7.
Connecticut's
Most Famous Ghost Towns
Location: Cornwall,
Pomfret, Hebron, Dudleytown

One of Connecticut's abandoned villages, Dudleytown is more famous, or should I say *infamous*, than many of its thriving cities and towns. Along with Dudleytown, Connecticut has two other renowned, though to a lesser extent than Dudleytown, lost villages: Bara Hack in Pomfret and Gay City in Hebron.

Since I was young, I was always enthralled by legendary tales of the unknown (which eventually led to the creation of this book!). I was told stories of Maud's Grave and the Black Dog of West Peak, but I had never heard of Dudleytown before. Eventually, when I did, it was described to me as a notoriously haunted abandoned village in the woods, which surely appealed to my seventeen-year-old self. My high school creative writing teacher clued me in on this fascinating place. He said he tried to venture to the lost village once when he was younger, but as he and his friends squeezed into the car to set out on the mission, the car ominously died. He took that as a foreboding sign and never actually set foot in what some call "Owlsbury," named after the plethora of owls found in the region.

I myself was never able to enter this village, either. My experience came while on the way home from college visits in upstate New York with my family. By this time, I had researched background information on Dudleytown and knew a decent amount about it. We were traveling Route 7 south from the Massachusetts Berkshires and stopped at a gas station at the confluence of Routes 4 and 7 in Cornwall Bridge for directions. Having the best intentions (exploring out of interest and not for the purpose of finding a party spot), and it being broad daylight, we figured this heightened our chances of visiting Dudleytown. We were wrong; even my mother, then in her fifties, could not break the staunch Yankee cashier's silence on how to find the lost village.

"Hello, could you please tell me where the entrance to Dudleytown is?" The answers ran the gamut from a feigned clueless response of "What are you talking about?" to a very protective "You don't go down in there!"

We set out toward home, disappointed that we were not able to visit Owlsbury ourselves, but felt our convictions were reaffirmed by the locals' steadfastness in not letting us know where Dudleytown was located. Ironically, I later found out that the gas station was only a stone's throw away from Dark Entry Road, which was a primary entrance to the former town.

The northwestern corner of Connecticut, also known as the Litchfield Hills, is marked by windy country roads, an abundance of wildlife, wooded hills, reclusive celebrities, and picturesque rivers and streams. Cornwall Bridge is a picture postcard example of many of these elements of Litchfield County. In 1738, the first settlers of European descent encroached on the lands eventually known as Dudleytown.

Nine years later, the first of the Dudley clan would settle in the Cornwall woods. By 1800, the Dudleytown section of Cornwall was flourishing with elements of a successful village, including homes, a meeting house, and a town hall. Some say that the Dudley family once had a curse placed upon them. Although historians may argue, part of the legend of Dudleytown harkens back to the day of the family's supposed ancestors across the pond in England. A distant relative, Edmund Dudley, was decapitated during the reign of Henry VIII. Another Dudley, John Dudley, was found plotting to have his son marry Lady Jane Grey, the temporary queen. Still another English Dudley brought with him a case of the plague while fighting in France, which in turn, wiped out thousands of English citizens. In no uncertain terms, the English Dudleys were not very popular.

Fast-forward to the Dudleys and other inhabitants of Dudleytown. Abiel Dudley died a pauper. Gershorn Hollister was killed at William Tanner's house, and as a result, William went mad. Dudleytown's Carter family decided to move to the area around Binghamton, New York. While Nathaniel Carter was temporarily out of the home, hostile Native Americans broke into the Carter homestead, cracked his wife's head in two with a tomahawk and bashed his baby's brains out on the wall. Nathaniel was the next in line; his fate was a scalping at Native American hands. Back in Dudleytown, the family of Nathaniel's brother, Adoniram, was wiped out by an illness. The curse of Dudleytown continued throughout the village including other residents being tragically killed, going insane, or suffering other calamities. The list included Mary T. Greely, wife of newspaperman and presidential nominee Horace Greely. She became insane and died after her husband lost the presidential bid. The last of Dudleytown's residents left in 1901 after his house burned down.

The village lay dormant for years until a New York doctor, William C. Clark, bought a tract of land to build a summer residence for himself and his wife. The couple vacationed in the Dudleytown woods happily for a few years until tragedy struck. Dr. Clark was called back to New York City on an emergency trip, and although his wife pleaded for him not to go, Clark reassured her that he would be back in less than two days. Upon his return, to his surprise, his normally loyal wife was not waiting for him at the train platform as prearranged. As he entered the house, there was still no sign of his wife, until unearthly sounds reverberated from the middle of his house. The manic laughter was caused by his wife who had somehow lost her mind during his brief visit to the city.

Pessimists will rule out Dudleytown's curse as simply bad luck, albeit terribly, horribly, no good, very bad luck at that! Others will cite the changing economy and changing personal lifestyles as the downfall of the town. Instead of working on family farms, many younger generations looked for opportunities in bigger cities and towns like New York City and Hartford. The more superstitious set, though, blames the curse for seemingly mysterious circumstances, like my teacher's car not starting on the outset of the trip and the tragedies befalling many in the town. Today, what remains of Dudleytown are cellars where dwellings once stood, although many visitors proclaim that more than stone still exists there. Visitors have heard strange noises and voices echoing through the woods. Others have seen odd lights and ghostly orbs, while some have even witnessed spectral figures floating amongst what was once the center of the thriving village.

Whether Dudleytown's demise came at the hands of a centuries-old curse or was the natural progression of a colonial settlement, Dudleytown remains today as one of the most talked about haunted locales in the nation. Dudleytown is on private land; visitors are not welcome.

Bara-Hack

Due east from Dudleytown lies Bara-Hack, another ghost town that is named for the Welsh term for "breaking bread." As with Dudleytown, it is yet another ghost town that I have been unsuccessful in finding. The directions to Bara-Hack are not quite precise. Bara-Hack is supposedly located in the Abington section of Pomfret, at the junction of Routes 44 and 97. Bara-Hack is located off of the first left on Route 97 north of the intersection. Here is where it gets tricky, though: it is down an unmarked side path. After a few unsuccessful trips wandering the paths that follow Mashmoquet Brook, I left empty-handed.

The village was started by two Welsh families around 1780. Just like Dudleytown, the town grew and prospered, but by 1890, all its residents had moved away or died. When the factory that was located in the village came to its demise, the town soon followed suit. Ironically, this town has become better known since its living residents have moved out. Bara-Hack is now nicknamed the "Village of Voices" due to the sounds that have not gone away, even though its population has left. Ever since the beginning of its existence, odd occurrences have been happening here. One particularly strange story recalled that slaves saw the phantasmal images of their dead masters relaxing in tree branches above the town cemetery. In the 1970s, an investigative team recorded dogs barking, laughing children, cows mooing, and people talking, although nothing or no one was present except the team, nature, and stone foundations. Many visitors have reported hearing similar sounds — sounds as if the daily life of the village was taking place and thriving in the 1800s. Echoing similar sentiment as the slaves, a modern account includes a sighting of a gentleman's bearded face rising above the cemetery and again figures reclining in the trees above the graveyard. Just like Dudleytown, Bara-Hack is located on private property and is off limits to the public.

Factory Hollow Village

This last ghost town *is* accessible to visitors. It is the former Factory Hollow Village in what today is called Gay City State Park. This village is located in Hebron. Its history is similar to the other villages, founded in the 1700s and abandoned by the late nineteenth century. However, this village's history has a bit of a twist. A focal point of the community was, not surprisingly, its religious services. Church in Factory Hollow consisted of praying to God, punctuated by cursing and drunken brawls fueled by the hard alcohol served during the religious ceremony. A woolen mill was erected in 1810, and although its tenure was not long, the town was supported by industry until the paper mill burned down in 1879. With the loss of the town's economic base, as well as a change in the populace's lifestyle, the older generation dying out, and many men lost to the Civil War, Factory Hollow, just like Dudleytown and Bara-Hack, faced its end. The land was turned into a state park in the mid 1900s, and named Gay City after one of the town's prominent families.

Gay City, or Factory Hollow, has a murderous past. A traveling salesmen or a peddler of some sort was murdered or "disappeared" and his goods were stolen. A skeleton was found in a charcoal pit soon after. Ever since then, an ethereal skeleton has been spotted floating above that charcoal pit.

Another tale of Gay City involves a boy who was running late for work at the blacksmith shop. The blacksmith became so peeved at the tardy young man that he cut the boy's head off! That will teach him to never be late again, oh wait... The blacksmith, or whoever the culprit may be, was never indicted for murder, but a ghost of a young boy who carries his head in his hands has been seen in the woods.

Similar to Bara-Hack, visitors have also reported hearing sounds as if the village were still thriving today.

Of the three villages, Factory Hollow is accessible to the public, since it is located on the grounds of present-day Gay City State Park. Foundations and cellars are what can be seen there now, as well as a small cemetery near the parking lot of the park. During my visit to Gay City, I found the cemetery, and although I did not see any ghostly decapitated figures, my dog enjoyed romping through the snow-covered trails. It's ironic that some of Connecticut's most fascinating towns are in ruins, perhaps inhabited by ghosts, and occasionally visited by dedicated history and folklore buffs.

Gay City State Park is located on Route 85 in Hebron.

A small cemetery located in the forgotten Factory Hollow settlement, known today as Gay City State Park.

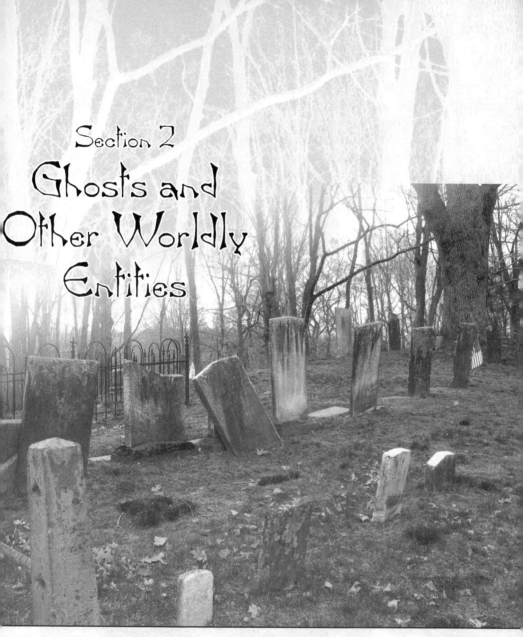

Section 2
Ghosts and Other Worldly Entities

Gravestones that have settled in various angles
at the old burial ground in Norwichtown

1.
The Bradley Playhouse
Location: Putnam

Old theaters tend to bring to mind images of ghosts and ghouls. For the vast majority of people who are used to going to the local multiplex housed in a concrete box, the idea of sitting in an ornately decorated antiquated theater is a little disorienting. Experiencing the range of emotions of live actors on stage, without the need for 3D glasses, is a much more personalized event. For some audience members and visitors to the Bradley Playhouse in Putnam, it is not only the living actors who provide theses thrills and chills; the theater itself has proved frequent and sometimes hair-raising entertainment.

Putnam is a former mill town that is finding some renaissance in its antique industry. Downtown Putnam, chock full of stores pitching their aged wares, is a lucky survivor among the forgotten mill towns of northeastern Connecticut. Although the boom economy of this mill town is still a distant past, Putnam has strong hints of revitalization. Bistros, a renovated train station (now a restaurant), and the majestic Bradley Theater, along with a plethora of antique stores, join the ranks of rehabilitated buildings in downtown Putnam.

Traveling past Bradley Playhouse today, the visitor can tell that the building oozes history. The idea of what is now called The Bradley was first conceived in 1890 by a local man named Ransom Bradley. He felt that the perfect Putnam should include a palace for the townspeople to witness national talent in a neighborhood location. Eleven years after the initial idea, The Bradley was completed on January 29, 1901, designed by a local man named Charles H. Kelley. At the time it was built, the theater was a state-of-the-art facility. It was equipped with such lavish features as carpets in a deep shade of red, a drinking fountain made of marble, a balcony, 973 opera chairs, and four boxes along the side of the theater. The heavy stage curtain was made of asbestos. The building, called different names over the years, was at one time known as the "Putnam Opera House." The opera house attracted national Broadway groups that took their talents to locations outside of the Big Apple. The theater soon after started showing silent movies, with a piano accompanying the moving picture. When "talkies" or movies with sight and sound came to The Bradley in 1928, it was the dawn of the modern theater, soon to be called "movie theater."

The Bradley was plagued by traumatic events, most notably three vicious fires that caused much damage to certain areas of the theater. In 1914, within the span of only fourteen hours, two fires rampaged through the theater. After these first two, the orchestra pit was covered and the balcony was renovated. In 1927, further remodeling was done to the Putnam Opera House, including an overhaul of the seats. The number of seats lessened, which benefited theater-goers due to extended leg room between rows so that the patrons could more comfortably enjoy themselves.

On December 9, 1937, more tragedy struck the Bradley. A blaze caused by a short-circuit in the dressing room engulfed much of the stage area. Luckily, the weighty asbestos curtain was lowered to trap the flames and confine it to the stage area. After withstanding three infernos in twenty-three years, the theater was lucky to still be standing. Throughout the twentieth century, The Bradley showed films and underwent many renovations (including an outstanding marquee over its doorway). Live theater returned to the building in the 1980s, with the current group, the Theatre of Northeastern Connecticut, establishing itself and taking residence there in 1991. Since then, the theater company has staged well-attended and critically acclaimed shows such as *The Boys Next Door, The Crucible,* and *A Christmas Carol.* With generous gifts to The Bradley, a new lighted marquee was installed, proudly welcoming the play-goer to a show at the Bradley.

In addition to having an interesting history, the Bradley Playhouse is one of the most haunted locations in Connecticut! It is home to several ghosts, none of which are believed to be of the malicious kind; they would rather play than cause harm. Actors and actresses performing at The Bradley have noticed many unusual occurrences. On the dressing room stairs, some have noticed a woman in a white dress, although when they turn the corner, she is no longer there. Another story involves a woman, who in the fire of 1937, jumped from the balcony onto the stage, although this story seems to conflict with the history of the building, since the fire broke out in, and was limited to, the stage area. One would think that she would not have wanted to jump *in* to the fire, but would instead be running *away* from it. Nevertheless, a woman who is connected in some way to the '37 fire is said to still be in the theater. Actors have also noticed one certain audience seat to be down, even when no one is sitting in it; it's hard to keep the seat down when it is a spring-loaded theater seat. Other cast members recall a heavy fire escape door slamming shut on a calm, windless night. These stories and more created such a reputation for The Bradley that it was even featured on an episode of *Ghost Hunters* in 2005!

Pat Green, the business manager of The Bradley since 1995, was gracious enough to be interviewed for this book. Pat gave her take on the theater's famous haunts. The Blue Lady is the most famous Bradley ghost. A volunteer named Bob claims to be psychic and sees the Blue Lady frequently. He says he knows her feelings, but cannot tell exactly how because she doesn't talk directly to him. Her name is Margaret and she wears a blue dress from the 1940s. She is straitlaced and does not like swearing, preferring upbeat musical shows. She hangs out in the balcony and leaves if she doesn't like the performance. A show that displeased her immensely was *Misery*, based on Stephen King's violent book about a disturbed fan who tortures a famous author. Some cast members claim to have seen a shadow or a vague figure in the balcony, but Bob is the most knowledgeable about the Blue Lady. Pat was skeptical about Bob's psychic abilities, but he once told her that her uncle "Ed something" was looking over her. She remembered that when she was a child, her Uncle Eddie died and there was no way that Bob could have known that name.

One Halloween season, the lobby was decorated like a haunted house, and when it was time to pick up items that people had lent the theater for the lobby, a woman came in to pick up her stuff. She entered the theater and sat for a while. After coming back into the lobby, she told Pat that there were eighty-three entities in the theater that could not move on to the next life, and that they were causing dissension among members of the theater troupe. She went home and a few days later Pat received an email that said, "Everything will be better now," because the woman had sent the entities on their way. A few weeks later, Bob, the usher, came into the theater and sat in a seat for three minutes. He came out into the lobby, distressed because he couldn't breathe, and said he had to leave. He returned a couple of weeks later, entered the theater again, and was visibly relieved. He said, "It's okay—they're back," referring to the four main ghosts who haunt The Bradley.

The four main ghosts are Margaret, the Lady in White (who traditionally haunts theaters), a boy, and a man.

A woman who calls herself the "Lightstream Lady" claims to have seen spirits in the theater. Her name is Carrie and she reads people's auras.

Another woman came to the theater and had a plum-bob (weight on a rope) attached to a string of beads. She attached the string of beads to Pat's arm and said, "If anyone is here, tell them to move the plum-bob." Pat did and it started moving. Pat says she was not consciously moving her arm. She then asked it to stop and it did. The weird thing was that it just stopped dead, no residual movement. This woman also went to the balcony railing, which only recently was renovated so that it was no longer knee-high, clutched her chest, screamed out, and sat down. She shrieked, "A child just fell over the balcony!" To Pat's knowledge there has never been a death in the theater, which is not to say that an injured person could not have died after being carried out of the theater. As an aside, Pat mentioned that kids have dropped numerous toys, shoes, etc. over the railing (especially when it was shorter) and the items have never hit anyone. They always fall in the aisle!

The famed ghost hunters, the Warrens, visited the theater and found it to be filled with energy.

Several actors have had paranormal experiences in the theater. One actress was in the lobby and the door to the office was closed. She and other staff members tried to get in and felt that it must be locked from the inside. It turns out that a very heavy safe had somehow been moved to block the door from the inside. Several actors have felt a hand on their shoulders on stage. Many will not go to the lower level or the dungeon (basement) alone, feeling that there's someone down there. Two children who had hung out at the theater with their parents since infancy have communicated with people who were not there. One of them claimed to be waving to the lady in the balcony. Pat's granddaughter said she saw a frog man on the stage. There was a rock on stage shaped like a bench, but the girl insisted that she saw a man squatting like a frog.

An actor sat down in one of the theater seats and felt someone sit next to him, but no one was there. He looked and there was an indentation in the seat of a person's rear end!

Pat Green was very kind in sharing some of her personal experiences. She claims that she never believed in paranormal activities, but that she has become more sensitive to the possibilities after a few events. She explains many of the sounds and sights scientifically. The building is old and creaky. It is really two buildings jammed together, with a small space in between, where the wind can be heard howling. There is glass covering the wall in the back of the theater, which reflects ghostly-looking images of real people. A couple of experiences have been a little disconcerting, however. One night, about 2 a.m., Pat was working in the office and heard footsteps in the lobby. She went out to the lobby, and although no one appeared, she suddenly felt very cold and realized that the hair was standing up on her arms. Another incident involved another thespian who was part of a cast of actors playing theater ghosts. Pat was on stage right and was chatting about ghosts with a couple of other actors. She made the statement, "There's no such thing as a ghost," at which point a screw gun fell off a paint can that was on a table on the stage—no wind, no one near it, weird!

Pat told these stories in a very straight-forward, matter-of-fact manner, and was rather wry at times. She said she never really feels frightened in the theater, even though she is often there alone, very late at night. She has never seen a ghost. During the conversation, her copy machine just turned itself on, and she did not seem to notice. In mentioning it later, she said that it was just resetting itself. The same thing happened with her computer. The lobby is quite opulent looking, with a 1940s aura. To enter the seating area, one goes through black curtains, which is a little creepy. A hazy figure that was seen turned out to be a living person reflected in an old mirror. Downstairs is where the dressing rooms are, as well as costumes. A lower level, called the dungeon, houses lots of props, including a rusty gurney from the 1950s. A fellow regional actor, who had visited the theater the previous week to borrow costumes, was quite creeped out by it. As Pat was talking, one of our group felt a pin prick in her derriere. She jumped and kind of made a joke about it, and felt around the costumes to see if any pins were sticking out. There were none. Pat continued with the tour and when she was finished the costumes were checked more thoroughly and found to have no pins. If it were a ghost (which seems too coincidental), it was probably a little poltergeist having fun.

For a building with such a storied past as the Bradley Playhouse has, it is understood why people just do not want to leave! Whether you visit the Bradley for a play, for a ghost sighting, or for its history, a trip to the antiquated theater is a must when visiting the northeast part of the state. With all this ghost activity, the name "quiet corner" will have to change!

Plan your visit to the playhouse during a run of one of their top-notch plays. If you happen to be watching a production of "A Christmas Carol," you may be able to see more ghosts than just the ones on stage!

Check out www.thebradleyplayhouse.com for more information. The theater is located at 30 Front Street in Putnam.

2.
Tales of Norwichtown
Location: Norwich

Norwichtown, the oldest section of the city of Norwich, is home to colonial era houses, an ancient burying ground, and a large town green. To begin this journey, let us start by a visit to Norwichtown in the ancient burial ground. Entering the graveyard from Old Cemetery Lane, a small road right off the Norwichtown Green, the visitor will arrive first in the older part of the burial ground. Impressive graves, which are relics of bygone colonial days with headstones depicting skulls and cherubs, have inscriptions warning readers to wisely put their time to use while on this earth and to be prepared! These words adorn the grave of a young man who died at age twenty-three:

This happy youth resigned his breath/ Prepared to live and ripe for death/
Ye blooming youth who see this none/ Learn early death to be your own.

An autumnal view of Norwichtown's Congregational Church taken from the Green.

Hannah Arnold

The grave with the most fanfare in the older section of the cemetery is that of Hannah Arnold, the mother of Norwich's most famous, or infamous, former citizen, Benedict Arnold. Although Ben is buried overseas in England (after he traded sides), legend says that he rides on his white steed each and every Halloween night at midnight to visit Mom. The cemetery is known to have patches of fog in it on otherwise clear nights. Hannah's son visiting her is not the only annual event to take place at her grave. Each year, someone leaves an offering of flowers and candles at the base of her gravestone.

Samuel Huntington

Crossing over the footbridge and into the "newer" half of the cemetery, the visitor is greeted by a large tomb. This newly renovated brick monument is the resting place of Samuel Huntington, former Governor of Connecticut and president of the Continental Congress. Being the first president of the Continental Congress, advocates, such as the now-deceased Norwich historian Bill Stanley, attest that Huntington should actually be recognized as the nation's first president. Huntington's tomb was restored in 2003. State archeologist Nick Bellantoni and his team examined the tomb and the contents inside. Part of the restoration included giving the deceased new coffins to rest in, as well as completely refurbishing the outside of the tomb. Bellantoni also observed that the Huntingtons were laid to rest in the buff, since clothes were too much of an expensive commodity at that time. History lesson aside, this tomb vaguely resembles a brick oven, the kind that could be used to make a crisp pizza... or bake a loaf of bread. Speaking of bread, the legend that surrounds Huntington's grave is that the smell of baking bread wafts through the air when visitors pay their respects.

Bela Peck

Up the main hill of the cemetery, on the right hand side, is the most noticeable of the graves in the burial ground. This one belongs to Bela Peck. Even though no direct legend is attributed to it, it is still worth a look since the face of his tombstone is held up by a stone hand placed atop Peck's monument, opening a scroll where his inscription is etched.

A walk through the adjoining Lowthorpe Meadow, the visitor may notice certain cold spots that happen out of nowhere, even on hot and balmy days. Noticeable cold spots are before crossing the bridge that leads to the Meadows Shopping Center and then on the other side of the meadows, near a stone bridge.

The older section of the burial ground in Norwichtown near the grave of Hannah Arnold.

Eerie Occurrences

Many of the houses located near the cemetery and around the green were built in the eighteenth century, and of those, some have had odd things happen in them. The Christoper Leffingwell Tavern, the Beebee and O'Neil Law Office, and the Samuel Abbot house are among those that have had eerie occurrences attributed to them.

The Samuel Abbot House

The Samuel Abbot House, built by a leathersmith in 1752, is a private residence that is located on East Town Street. One visitor to the house had an experience that even thirty years later, she cannot forget. Diana Silva of Irvington, New Jersey, was in Norwich, visiting friends at the Abbot house. The unforgettable event happened one night as she was sleeping in the guest bedroom, just as she was closing her eyes for the evening. She was lying on the bed, face down, when all of a sudden she had the sensation of someone else being in the room with her. The feeling got stronger and it was as if the person were leaning over her. She hesitantly turned over and looked up to see an extremely tall person hovering over her bed! It was a man dressed in a black suit. She describes the man as having a "long, thin face, hollow cheek bones," and the most vivid details she remembered were his eyebrows. "His eyebrows were shaped like little triangles," Silva recalls. Even though he did not speak, his facial expression and body language seemed to convey the message, "Don't be afraid, we are just curious." We? Yes, Silva said that he was not alone in the guest bedroom. The room was crowded, but other than the hovering man, she could only distinctly make out the shape and visage of a woman. She was also dressed in black, wearing a full-skirted dress, and was crying. Silva's recollection was so detailed that she remembered the woman wearing a lace doily on her head, reminiscent of the kind that Mary Todd Lincoln would wear. Silva said that she did not feel these were evil spirits, just extremely sad and inquisitive as to who she was and why she was in their room.

She remembered that after the experience, instead of crying out in distress, she simply drifted into sleep, a deep sleep. Her overall impression was that she was present at a wake. The scene was a room where someone had recently died, or possibly the people she saw were in a pronounced period of mourning. Silva felt honored to be able to see this realm.

In addition to the scene of mourning, the Samuel Abbot house has a few other ghostly experiences attributed to it. Around the same time period, deep moaning was heard in the living room—discomforting enough to make one visitor leave! A few years later, a child's tub toys were strewn all over the bathroom after the family was away for the evening.

A newspaper clipping that was found in the attic of the house brought attention to the grounds behind it. The land behind the Abbot house consists mostly of swamp. The newspaper clipping circa 1890 read that one man killed another in those woods, and gruesomely decapitated him. Investigators were able to locate the body, but the head was never recovered.

Another time the family was sitting in the living room and started to hear a tapping sound on glass from the kitchen. When they went to investigate the noise, they noticed that their dog had broken from her chain outside. They were able to retrieve her, went back into the house, and noticed there was a glass with a spoon inside it. Was the ghost signaling to them that the dog had gotten loose?

The most recent instance of paranormal activity in the house was witnessed in the mid-eighties. Have the spirits become accustomed to the inhabitants or are they merely taking a break?

While You're There:

Benny's

Although technically a chain, a can't miss stop while you are in Norwichtown is Benny's. Benny's is a home, automotive, toy, and *anything else that you need* store that has locations in southern Massachusetts, eastern Connecticut, and Rhode Island. The "Benny's scent" hits you as soon as the sliding doors welcome you into the bike section. The smell, a hint of rubber from the bicycles and tire section, mixed with other unknown odors create a concoction simply known as Benny's scent, truly intoxicating. Benny's is a refreshing alternative to the large chain stores, as it is more navigable, less stress provoking and provides a more personal shopping experience. It is a store where you can buy a highly desired toy for the kid, a new iron, or car accessories. As my late grandmother would say, "If Benny's doesn't sell it, you don't need it."

Benny's in Norwichtown is located at 33-35 New London Turnpike.

3.
Mystic Seaport's
Schaeffer Spotter Tavern
Location: Mystic

Why might you ask, in a book featuring off-the-beaten-path places in Connecticut, is there a chapter dedicated to one of the state's most popular tourist attractions? Well, plain and simple, it's haunted! Mystic Seaport is a living history museum located on the banks of the Mystic River. The workers don colonial era garb and explain to the visitors the art of blacksmithing, boat building, and other such professions practiced at the recreated village. Also on site is the steamship *Sabino*, a riverboat, that departs the Seaport for a small cruise of the Mystic River and downtown. The Seaport's biggest draw is its fleet of ships, most notably the *Charles W. Morgan*, which ghosts have been associated with, as well. The buildings in the Seaport, for the most part, have been relocated from other places. Many are authentic from the time period. Some of the Seaport buildings have ghost stories attached to them, including reports of shadowy figures walking on top of the windows of a building and the spirit of a gentleman in a top hat frequenting the print shop. However, the most "haunted" Seaport building is its tavern.

The Schaeffer Spotter Tavern is a building whose ghost likes to make its presence felt quite often. Named after the tavern in *Moby Dick*, visitors can try historic foods and wash them down with a Mystic Seaport beer or a cream soda. Ironically, the most haunted building on the grounds is a re-creation, built only in 1956, but features genuine period furnishings. Each and every day, before and after the onslaught of tourists, the staff has to make sure each of their respective parts of the village is left in tip-top shape. This means scrubbing, cleaning, dusting, organizing, making sure that everything is ready for the next busy day. The workers of the tavern seem to be doing double the amount of work though, for someone, or *something*, likes to rearrange items to suit their own taste!

At night, Mystic Seaport is patrolled by security who look for any strange happenings and make sure no one tries to get a free, after-hours visit. The workers of each location have to give the on-duty security guard the keys to their buildings before they leave for the night. Some mornings, though, the tavern staff come into a building that was not arranged exactly the way it was left the evening before. In one instance, whatever was in the tavern overnight decided to move candlesticks and take chairs that were put up, down. One staff member even remembers thoroughly dusting before she left the previous night, only to find the dust back with hand prints in it the next morning.

A boss at the tavern received a call one night from security complaining that someone was either in the tavern blasting music or someone had forgotten to turn it off before they left. The boss knew that neither was the case. Strange occurrences like the aforementioned ones tended to happen once or twice a week. Many people who visit the tavern say they feel a certain spirit in it. There is even a room in the upstairs that is padlocked and no one is allowed inside. Other than the dust incident, the ghost usually prefers to tidy up, rather than make a mess. It likes to fix pictures that were crooked on the wall, and moves items from the bar to the table, or from the table to the mantle. Rumor has it that there may be photographic proof of a Seaport spirit tucked away somewhere in the files of the museum.

So the next time friends from out of town want to go visit Mystic Seaport, a place you've visited numerous times, this time go with your eyes peeled for what might happen behind the scenes.

Mystic Seaport is located at 275 Greenmanville Avenue in Mystic (Route 27). The Seaport is one of the state's top attractions and can be very busy, especially in the summer time. The admission at the time of this writing was $24 for adults. It can be a full day's event.

While You're There:

Stonington Borough

Visit Stonington Borough. Mystic is actually a village that is part of two towns: Stonington and Groton. Downtown Mystic, which is hardly off the beaten path, is full of shops and restaurants. Located on Route 1-A, east of Mystic, is Stonington Borough. The Borough, although another enclave of restaurants, shops, and galleries, is less tourist-filled and features hidden gems like the Water Street Café and Zack's Bar and Grille. Old captains' houses and seaside homes hug close together along the tiny streets. At the tip of the village is the Stonington Historical Society's Old Lighthouse Museum. The stone lighthouse became a museum in 1927. The adjacent parking lot is a peninsula that sticks out into Fishers Island Sound. A trip here is worth it, even if only for this majestic view of the ocean on three sides. On the left, visitors can see the end of Rhode Island's Watch Hill and Napatree Point.

4.
Two Ghosts of the Elm City
Location: New Haven

New Haven, the Elm City, is known for Yale University, amazing pizza, and top-notch theater. It is also home to a number of resident ghosts. These two tales come from opposite ends of the city. The first story takes place on Saltonstall Avenue, in the eastern part of New Haven. It is located in a mostly residential neighborhood, with multi-family homes, churches, and restaurants. This is an account from Laurie Knitter, a former resident of a multi-family house on Saltonstall Avenue. This story takes place during her tenure in the dwelling, during the late '80s, around the year 1989.

Laurie said that one night she was watching television on her living room couch around 11 p.m. From the couch, she could clearly see the entire kitchen. The living room and kitchen lights were off, but there was a light on in the bathroom that was next to the kitchen that shed light into it. As she was watching TV, she thought she noticed her husband standing at the refrigerator with the door open, but was curious, since she thought he had gone to bed hours before. With a closer look at the figure in the refrigerator doorway, she noticed it was whitish, had loose-fitting clothing, and was very thin. She could tell it was a man and presumably thought it was her husband because he fit that description and also wore pajamas like the figure was wearing. When Laurie called to ask if her "husband" was all right, the figure turned towards her, crumpled to the floor, and suddenly disappeared. The door that "he" had opened automatically closed, as refrigerator doors do.

Laurie was too far away with inadequate light to make out the facial expression of the figure. Her reaction to the incident was, "It was as if he saw me, I scared him, and he got out of there the fastest way he could." She then rushed over to her bedroom to find her husband fast asleep in the bed. She went to the refrigerator, but nothing was moved and nothing felt particularly cold or warm in the area where the figure was spotted. Laurie said that she did not feel fear, mostly because the figure looked so young and that she felt that she scared it more than it scared her!

A few months later, as Laurie and her husband were getting ready to move out, she mentioned this story to her landlord. Her expectation was that the landlord would laugh the matter off or pay it no mind. Surprisingly, instead the landlord said that he also had felt presences in the building when he was refurbishing it earlier. One instance he recalled was a time that he was working on a ladder in the basement while doing work on the electrical system. As he was on top of the ladder, he turned and saw a black shadow of some kind and then felt the shadow, or whatever it was, swoop through him. This incident was more menacing than Laurie's. The landlord mentioned that previous owners included a mother and father with their bachelor son living upstairs. Laurie feels that the figure that she saw may have been this young man. Did Laurie see the spirit of the young bachelor returning to his former home? Or was it someone else, from years earlier? The house on Saltonstall Avenue is currently a private home.

Evergreen Cemetery

A more well-known New Haven haunt takes place at the other end of the city. Evergreen Cemetery, a large modern cemetery located in a residential section of the western end of New Haven, is home to New Haven's most notorious specter, Midnight Mary. Not much is known about Mary E. Hart during her lifetime. Some say that she led a normal, unassuming life. What *is* known is the ominous inscription etched upon her pink, marble grave:

AT HIGH NOON, JUST FROM, AND ABOUT TO RENEW HER DAILY WORK, IN HER FULL STRENGTH OF BODY AND MIND, MARY E. HART, HAVING FALLEN PROSTRATE: REMAINED UNCONSCIOUS, UNTIL SHE DIED AT MIDNIGHT, OCTOBER 15, 1872, BORN DECEMBER 16, 1824

Written above her information in an arc, is the inscription "The People Shall Be Troubled At Midnight and Pass Away." This statement on her pink gravestone standing out among the others at this cemetery have led to numerous legends attributed to Mary and her gravesite. One legend says that Midnight Mary was *thought* to be dead, but was actually not. She was mistakenly buried alive! Another popular tale is that Mary shows up on the side of the road, hitchhiking of sorts. According to David Philips's *Legendary Connecticut,* Mary would ask a driver to drop her off at "home," which is on Winthrop Avenue. This is the road that abuts Evergreen Cemetery, and Mary's grave can be seen from it. Phillips also says that there are stories of college students camping out overnight at her grave who never return from their visit. In doing further research, the seemingly ominous inscription is actually taken from the Book of Job in the Bible. The full sentence from the Bible reads:

In a moment shall they die, and the people shall be troubled at midnight, and pass away: and the mighty shall be taken away without hand.

Was Mary Hart just a regular citizen of New Haven whose gravestone inscription caused much unwarranted speculation as to who she was, or is the stone truly an indicator of the paranormal incidents caused by Mary? If it is because of the inscription, Bible verses are commonplace on stones, but taken out of context, the passage does seem threatening. However she is viewed, three simple words, "died at midnight," have given Mary E. Hart the nickname "Midnight Mary" for all of eternity.

During my visit to look for the stone of Midnight Mary, we traversed the edge of Evergreen Cemetery by car until we found the pink rectangular marker. Unfortunately, the only entrance to the cemetery is on Ella Grasso Boulevard, directly on the other side. Once we were able to spot the stone from the street, it was easy to trace the path inside the cemetery to the Winthrop Street side. If there were no legend associated with Mary Hart's resting place, the part of the cemetery where she is buried would seem ordinary. Without having previous knowledge of stories, the color of the stone and the inscription do catch your eye. Other than that, nothing stands out, as the burial ground is in a well lit and oft-traveled section of New Haven.

The cemetery is relatively new and borders a residential neighborhood lined with houses and Ella Grasso Boulevard, which is full of businesses and has a constant flow of traffic. The cemetery is close to the intersection of Routes 1 and 10 in New Haven.

While You're There:

Yale Peabody Museum of Natural History

Visit the Yale Peabody Museum of Natural History. If you think New Haven's ghosts are ancient, you must not have visited this museum. Full of dinosaur skeletons, the Peabody attracts young and old alike. The museum also houses dioramic depictions of Connecticut outdoor scenes, an Ancient Egypt display, and a revolving exhibit hall. It is small enough to be manageable for kids, but big enough to hold their interest.

The Peabody is located 170 Whitney Avenue in New Haven.

5.
Nathan Hale Homestead
Location: Coventry

Connecticut's state hero, who proclaimed the famous line, "I regret that I only have one life to live for my country," was Nathan Hale. He was a school teacher, a patriot, and a spy. Born and raised in Coventry, he was educated at Yale and taught school in New London and East Haddam. Although called the Nathan Hale Homestead, Nathan never lived there, although many generations of Hales did. It is a historical and paranormal landmark.

Nathan Hale was born in Coventry in 1755. He attended Yale at age 14 and graduated at 17. He was a school teacher, who joined the Continental Army as first sergeant of the local militia, became a captain, and, later, America's first spy. He was part of a team of Special Forces under Colonial leader Thomas Knowlton known as "Knowlton's Rangers." Hale was suspected as a spy while he was guised as a Dutch teacher, and was ratted out by loyalists in a tavern in New York. He was reported to British General Howe, and before he was hanged, uttered his famous line. The Hale family was already known in Colonial American history, as his grandfather was John Hale, a judge who eventually spoke out against witchcraft in Beverly, Massachusetts, after being one of the interviewers at the Salem Witch Trials.

The Hales purchased the Coventry house lot in 1740. The family had twelve children and the home had crop fields and livestock. The current Hale Homestead was built in 1776, a large home in the Georgian style. The family moved in a month after Nathan was hanged. The Hales inhabited the home until the early 1800s.

Time went on, and in 1913 the house was vacant. An attorney and historian from New Haven named George Dudley Seymour bought the house. In the back of the house, near the barn and current visitor's center, is a large tower-shaped pile of stones, which is a memorial to his own beloved horse. It was George Seymour who proposed that Hale become Connecticut's state hero.

Today, the visitor can tour the home on a guided visit. The inside is furnished with period pieces. It has paintings of family members on its walls. Visitors can go into a secret passageway that Nathan's father would have used, entering into the adjoining workroom as a justice of the peace. George Seymour dined with guests such as John Singer Sargent and President William Howard Taft here. Visitors are able to venture into bedrooms, the kitchen, and living areas.

On the paranormal side of things, guides have reported seeing light in the attic windows. There have been strange shadows gliding across rooms. During one ghost hunt, EVPs were even caught on tape.

While You're There:

Bidwell Tavern

Although at the Nathan Hale House you may see something that is other-worldly, down the road at the Bidwell Tavern you can taste something that is truly out of this world. A stop here is a must for any fan of chicken wings. With about thirty styles including Hickory Smoked, Green Mountain, and Cajun Honey BBQ, the array of flavors outnumbers most wing establishments tenfold. The tavern has existed for well over a hundred years, and with food this good, will be around for 100 more!

Bidwell is at 1260 Main Street in Coventry.

6.
Diana's Pool
Location: Chaplin

Diana's Pool is located in the Goodwin Nature Preserve in Chaplin, which was purchased by James Goodwin in 1951 for $11,000. Chaplin, as well as other nearby towns, signed a compact agreeing to protect this property. The Natchaug River, which in the past provided power for several mills, runs through the property. Now the area is used for recreational purposes, including trout fishing. Swimming is prohibited, although the signs are often ignored. It is a short walk from the parking area to the river, which is frequently tested and found to be pristine. The setting is beautiful, reminiscent of rivers and streams in Vermont, with several small rapids bubbling over rocks like mini-waterfalls. The river widens to form the area called Diana's Pool, surrounded by high rock walls. In the summer, people jump off a cliff into the pool with a depth of fifteen feet in some places. A few years back, after several days of rain, a grandmother took her grandchildren to look at the river. Sadly, the grandmother was washed away and drowned.

Legends

There are a few legends associated with Diana's Pool.
1. This has been confirmed. A family with the last name Diana owned the pool and ran a concession stand near it—some say in the 1800s and some say in the 1930s and 1940s.
2. Kids from the town of Hampton named the pool after Diana, the goddess of love.
3. A heartbroken young woman named Diana jumped off the cliff on an icy night and died. When the moon is full, legend is that she can still be heard crying today.
4. The last is a variation of the third story, except that the young woman was crying and fell into the river by slipping on her own tears.

The Natchaug River in Chaplin formed this natural swimming hole that today is known as Diana's Pool.

7.
Legendary
Connecticut All-Stars
Locations: Easton, Winchester, and Burlington

The three following stories are the pinnacle of the Connecticut legend genre. I was tempted not to even include them, since the stories are so prevalent in the state's folklore. My mind was changed when talking with a good friend who told me that in this collection, these stories MUST be included. I made a compromise of sorts; instead of dedicating a whole chapter to each, I condensed these three into a single entry.

The Green Lady

The first story takes place due west of Hartford, in the town of Burlington, which might be considered a buffer between the metro-capital region and the bucolic Litchfield Hills. This is the story of the Green Lady, a mostly benign ghost who resides in a small, stonewall enclosed cemetery, located just far enough off of the main road on a less traveled dirt road. The Green Lady is the ghost of Elisabeth Palmiter, a woman who lived close to the cemetery and drowned in a nearby swamp, either mysteriously or when her husband was unable to save her — depending on the variation. People who have witnessed Elisabeth say that she is beautiful, shrouded in a green mist presumably from the swamp water. Visitors to the cemetery feel strange emotions while paying respects to Elizabeth, and oftentimes extra images will show up in photographs that were not seen by the naked eye!

In David Philips's *Legendary Connecticut,* accounts by his students at Eastern Connecticut State University warned of two large oaks in the cemetery that people have crashed into because of Elisabeth. They also cautioned women to cut their fingernails before entering the cemetery or they might become possessed by the Green Lady. The students mentioned a portrait of Elisabeth, hanging in the window of a nearby house that always seemed to have its shades pulled open. Phillips calls the Green Lady "Connecticut's most boring ghost" and because of her anonymity, tales have been embellished to present this haunt as menacing.

My trips to the Seventh Day Baptist Cemetery on Upson Road, a small dirt road off of Covey Road, have been less than fruitful. I have not witnessed firsthand any supernatural sightings or experienced strange emotions. Due to vandalism and Mother Nature, many stones in this cemetery have been toppled, but Elisabeth's stone remains standing. Elisabeth's gravestone was adorned with a rose when I visited in the spring of 2001, and with pennies when I went back in the fall of 2009. The location of the cemetery is truly a perfect place for a ghost story. Upson Road is not far off CT Route 4, but still retains a rural feel.

When I visited, I did not see any houses in close proximity, and none of the homes located farther up the road had curtains open to reveal a picture of the Green Lady. The story about the oaks proved to be false as well, since the tale stated that motor vehicle operators were driving into the cemetery, which is not possible, since it is a tiny graveyard with no driving lanes.

The Winsted Wildman

A few miles farther into the northwest woods of the state lies the town of Winchester. Winsted, a section of Winchester, is a popular viewing spot for a large, hairy apeman, nicknamed by locals "The Winsted Wildman." This Bigfoot of the Litchfield Hills was first recorded with a sighting by the then selectman Riley Smith. While en route to Colebrook, Riley stopped to pick blueberries along the way and was astonished to see a naked, hairy beast-man dash by him. This story, from 1895, was the first sighting of what would become a somewhat frequent occurrence.

In 1895, a handful of other locals reported seeing the Wildman. One theory was that the "creature" was actually a local painter named Arthur Beckwith who had recently escaped from a mental hospital and was on the lam. The painter was sent to the Litchfield Asylum after suffering a traumatic accident. Two years after he was sent away, he escaped and was found in Cuba, naked, eating raw meat and vegetables. Even though he was harmless, he created quite a stir. When he was discovered, he was then taken back to Litchfield, but was transferred to Sanford Hall Sanitarium in Flushing, Queens, New York. He escaped again in 1894! Could Mr. Beckwith have been the Winsted Wildman?

Fast forward about seventy years, and the Wildman is on the loose again! Near Crystal Lake Reservoir, two boys watched a hairy, tall, and naked man-beast from their window. In 1974, two years later, two couples that were "parking" had a run-in with the Wildman. The startled teens reported their findings to the police, but by the time the police arrived, the elusive Wildman was gone!

The White Lady

The last story in this trilogy is Connecticut's most famous haunted locale, and that by some has been proclaimed as the most haunted sight in the entire nation. Famous Connecticut-based ghost hunters Ed and Lorraine Warren frequented this spot and even wrote an entire book about it, entitled *Graveyard*. The place is Union Cemetery in Easton, a rural town nestled directly above Fairfield, and the ghost is the world-famous White Lady.

Union Cemetery is an otherwise nondescript classic New England cemetery, located right next to a white church and surrounded by an iron fence at the intersection of Routes 136 and 59. At night, Union Cemetery has been the scene of orbs, ghostly mists, and actual ghost sightings.

The White Lady's actual identity is unconfirmed, but there is much speculation to who she was. Some say she was a mother who died during childbirth, eternally searching for her child. Others say she could be a woman who was killed after her husband had been murdered and whose body was thrown behind the church. Another theory is that her name is Ellen Smather, and her stalker killed her husband in hopes that Ellen would fall in love with him. When Ellen did not comply, he killed her as well and threw her body into the sinkhole behind the church. Yet another theory is that the White Lady is the ghost of a woman who was murdered by her adulterous lover.

Whatever the true reason for her demise, it is clear that she is still around in some form. Ed Warren even got footage of her on film (which has never been released to the public). She has been depicted as a woman in her 30s, with black hair, wearing a white nightgown. Warren described seeing the White Lady come towards him, but she was held back by shadow ghosts that were pulling at her as she walked.

Numerous spooky stories surround not only this cemetery, but also Stepney Cemetery, which is just up the road in the Stepney section of Monroe. The White Lady has been seen there, too. A local fireman even hit her with his car, and when he went to check out what had happened, no one was there, but there was a dent in the car! Another local man, on the way home from work in the early hours of the morning, felt that someone was with him in his car. He looked over and saw a hat-wearing, stubble-faced man sitting next to him. Looking back at the road, he saw a lady in the distance, and when he glanced back in his passenger seat, the man was gone! The woman was sticking her hand out and he ended up driving through her. If this was not enough, his lane of the road turned a cranberry red as he was driving past the cemetery. It finally dissipated when he was at the bottom of the next hill.

The White Lady likes to make her presence known after midnight, often even later between 1 and 3 a.m., which is unfortunate since the Easton police like to make their presence known in that same area during that same time. She has caused quite a furor over the years, and trespassers will be faced with arrests, fines, and altogether unwanted repercussions.

I have visited and driven by Union Cemetery many times in the last ten or so years and have sadly never witnessed anything horrifying or supernatural. Unlike my usually skeptical good friend who claims to have seen orbs and mists surrounding photos of a young man in the graveyard, I have walked through the grounds during the day and have driven around the perimeter at night and have experienced nothing out of the ordinary.

8.
Historic and Haunted Woodstock
Location: Woodstock

Woodstock is a quintessential New England village nestled into the northeast corner of Connecticut (although it was originally incorporated as part of Massachusetts). Its major thoroughfare is Route 169, which, along with the Merritt Parkway, is one of two national scenic byways in the state. It is home every Labor Day weekend to the Woodstock Fair, a classic agricultural extravaganza with rides for the kids, livestock demonstrations, and copious amounts of fried food for everyone. Woodstock paints a magnificent picture most impressively during the autumn months, where red, yellow, and gold overhang the town streets. In the same seasonal vein, Woodstock is home to antique stores and the Christmas Barn, which, hence the name, specializes in Christmas décor, but also has much autumn memorabilia as well.

Although Woodstock creates a vivid, sentimental scene, that is not the primary concern of this book! Smack dab in the center of town is the large town green, surrounded by homes stunning in their architecture, a church, a cemetery, and the town's institution of higher learning, Woodstock Academy.

Woodstock Academy

The main Academy building looks out majestically onto the green as if it were protecting the town from outsiders. It is a wooden, three-storied, beige Victorian building that was built in 1873. The Academy itself was founded in 1801. Legend goes that about 100 years ago, a headmaster of the Academy hanged himself in the building. According to one librarian of Woodstock Academy, he has not completely left!

Ghostly happenings occur in the library building that is located to the right of the main building. The librarian said that many days between 5 and 5:30, she sees a flash of light, described as a "shadow with force," dash across the library from left to right (while facing building).

The building that now houses the library was built in 1886, and at one time housed the Academy's gymnasium and cafeteria. The haunting started around 2009, when the second floor of the library was built. Every once in a while, the librarian still gets an uneasy feeling that the former headmaster is still there.

Legend tells of a former headmaster committing suicide in the main building of Woodstock Academy.

A Hutch-Moving Ghost

Woodstock is home to other haunts, including one house where its resident ghost did not like where the owner of the house placed her hutch. Once the hutch was moved, the ghost would move it back. On one Christmas morning, it even put the silverware away!

Roseland Cottage

One of Woodstock's main attractions is the peculiar "pink house," officially called the Roseland Cottage. This was the summer home of Henry Bowen, a wealthy New York merchant, publisher, and abolitionist. At this home, Bowen's house guests included every president from Ulysses S. Grant through William McKinley. Bowen loved roses (hence the hue of his home) and 4th of July. Roseland Cottage had extensive Independence Day celebrations marked by impressive fireworks displays. The house was built in the Carpenter Gothic Revival style, with pronounced arches, shutters, peaks, and stained glass. The property also includes one of the country's oldest bowling alleys, an ice house, a summer house, a large barn, and an aviary. On the grounds of the Roseland Cottage is a boxwood garden. Boxwood are short green shrubs often used as boundary placements.

Today, the Roseland Cottage is open to the public from June to mid-October. It is home to Civil War reenactments, an annual popular arts and crafts festival, and outdoor concerts. Tours are given on the hour. To get tickets for tours or more information, visit the barn that is located at the back of the property.

The center of Woodstock is located on Route 169 in the northernmost section of Connecticut's Quiet Corner.

While You're There:

Woodstock Orchards

For crisp apple cider and fall pumpkins, check out Woodstock Orchards, a short walk from the Woodstock Green. For more seasonal fun, take the quick trip up the road to the Christmas Barn, which is full of crafts and holiday décor. During the Quiet Corner's "Walktober," walks detailing Woodstock's history are commonplace. Walktober is an extensive series of guided walks, sponsored by The Last Green Valley, through various corners of the eastern part of the state which take place yearly in the month of October.

9.
Devil Comes to East Haddam
Location: East Haddam

The Devil must have spent much time in Connecticut. Places with diabolical names are as common as Volvos. From Weston to Montville, Sterling to New Hartford, no corner of the state stands unscathed from the wrath of the Dark One. The stories behind these places are as varied as the towns that contain them. One of the most demonic stories comes from a stretch of woods in central Connecticut known as Devil's Hopyard.

Devil's Hopyard

A few miles off the state road Route 82 in East Haddam, Connecticut, standing tall is Chapman Falls, the 60-foot roaring waterfall that is the highlight of the 860-acre wooded Devil's Hopyard State Park. This part of the park is known for its plentiful trout, a spectacular array of birds, and devilish figures playing violins at the top of the falls.

Sightings of Satan and other demons near and around Chapman Falls are one of the possible reasons for this park's diabolical name (Devil's Hopyard).

Over time, potholes formed in the rocks at the base of the falls, which scientists say were created from years of water erosion. But maybe they are wrong. Early settlers claimed that Satan could be seen rosining his bow at the top of the falls, while the witches of Haddam stirred a gruesome broth in the potholes. The potholes themselves were formed when the Devil took a tumble and his tail scorched the rocks during his downward spiral into the river below.

Other Legends of Hopyard

Other stories emerge from this diabolical place. A misled youth who, to play a trick on his minister father, dressed in a bull's hide and horns, was mistaken for Satan himself.

Another legend involves a man named Dibble, who owned the hopyard in the present park area. A hopyard is a place where hops, one of the four main ingredients in beer, are grown. The word *Dibble* sounds quite like *Devil*. (So maybe Dibble's Hopyard was misconstrued for Devil's Hopyard?) Dibble was also accused of distilling his own liquor, and freely handing it out to anyone who was thirsty, including children. He got the nickname "Devil" from their disapproving mothers. The legend of Dibble, though, has no historical evidence.

No one knows the true reason why this area of woods in East Haddam has been named Devil's Hopyard, but over the years, this area has seen its share of alleged Satanic or supernatural encounters, the most recent being five men who in 1999 said they were pursued by demons during their time in the Hopyard.

This park has many natural attractions to offer its visitors, more than those just hopeful to catch a glimpse of Satan. There are camp grounds, picnic tables by the river, trails for hikers, and the beautiful falls often captured by photographers. So if you are in the mood for some outdoor fun, Devil's Hopyard State Park is a good choice to bring the dog (allowed on a leash), the kids, and your local troop of Satanists.

Devil's Hopyard is located at 366 Hopyard Road in East Haddam

10.
Demonic Possession
Location: Bozrah

For such a small town where the population is barely 2,000, Bozrah certainly has its share of strange tales of murders, hideous beasts, and even UFO sightings. While Bozrah's better known stories, like the Irving-Johnson murder and the Sunken House of Gardner Lake, took place decades ago, this story is from the present day.

Bozrah is comprised mainly of wooded land, with the exception of the three small villages of Gilman, Fitchville, and Leffingwell. Even though this region of the state is populated by colonial dwellings, this story takes place in a newer house, built only in the 1980s, on land that was once part of the vast wilderness of Bozrah.

A young woman in her twenties had been living in her Bozrah home since she was born, only a few short years after the house was built by her father. Ashley, now the mother of a young child, continues to live in her childhood home with her mom. The home was always welcoming, with its meticulously placed furniture and its country home décor. Compared to many of the houses in the area, it was new, with modern amenities, a finished basement, and spacious rooms. Ashley's family is the only family that has lived in the house, so there was no question about what life was like in the house before they moved in.

One night in midsummer 2011 the serenity of the house suddenly stopped. It began when Ashley's son, Greg, always a docile and agreeable youngster, started throwing temper tantrums. The tantrums peaked one night when Ashley was trying to put him to bed. As she was putting him to sleep, he loudly objected, "No go to sleep." From her room, Ashley could clearly hear the tantrum continuing and decided it would be best to bring her son into the bedroom with her. After a while, Ashley decided to put him back into his crib and let him sleep there, for the benefit of both parties.

At 11 p.m., Greg started screaming, "Lights on, want lights on." Ashley was concerned, for his bouts of fussiness had never taken on such longevity or intensity. Ashley brought Greg downstairs to figure out what was troubling him and to try and calm him down. Once she got her son downstairs, Greg started flailing his arms and legs wildly in all kinds of awkward ways. The craziness did not stop there, for he then proceeded to do a back flip. In front of her own two eyes she witnessed her two-year-old son do a back flip! He was spinning around, mumbling incoherent phrases under his breath that sounded like he was speaking another language. Ashley, completely baffled as to what to do, and incredibly scared, yelled for her mother to come help her out. Ashley and her mom were shaking and poking him, trying to do anything they could to get him to snap out of this fit.

This is when Ashley and her mom noticed that Greg's eyes, usually bright blue and full of childhood wonder, were now glazed over and empty. Greg was not himself; the loving child was angry and did not even know who Ashley or his grandmother were. Under this trance, Greg knew the word "daddy" when normally that word was not part of his vocabulary. The spinning, babbling, and flailing lasted for about forty-five minutes until his grandmother, running out of options, splashed water on him. As soon as the water hit his skin, he immediately snapped out of this state and said, "Oh Mama, I love you."

Completely dumbfounded and terrified, Ashley took Greg to the doctor as soon as her sleepless night ended. Ashley explained to the doctor in detail the events of the night before. After reviewing the story and examining the child, the doctor ruled out a seizure or other medical maladies.

Ashley was at a loss. She had just witnessed her son spinning wildly and speaking a foreign language, and the visit to the doctor proved to be a dead end. She knew of an older Native American woman who worked with spirits. Ashley felt desperate, so she decided to speak with her. After hearing the story, the Native American woman had many questions for Ashley. The woman believed that Greg was experiencing some kind of otherworldly possession. She said that age two was the perfect time for possession. She also said that spirits are especially attracted to children with blond hair and blue eyes, and Greg had both. She also felt that there was some kind of sadness or bereavement associated with Ashley. She asked if anything especially sad, like a traumatic accident, had happened to Ashley or was associated with the house.

Ashley recalled a situation that happened when she was around Greg's age. A neighborhood boy came over to their house unannounced to play. He ended up spitting on her older brother, and Ashley's mother told the boy to never come back to their house. Later that day, the boy was tragically hit by a car and killed outside of his own home. When the Native American woman heard the story, she immediately felt that the spirit of the little boy could be possessing young Greg.

Over the next few days, Greg continued to behave strangely at times. For seemingly no reason, he would start shouting "No, no, no." Battery-powered toys were starting and stopping by themselves, lights were turning on and off. The woman who was in touch with spirits attributed this to the deceased neighborhood boy. Just like children in the flesh, spirits of the young enjoy toys, technology, and general mischief. From an acquaintance who practiced Wicca, Ashley was given remedies against negative spirits, including crystals and a sage packet. She was told to light the sage in different parts of the house. When the lit sage was placed underneath Greg's crib, it automatically blew out.

Another peculiar event happened involving a crystal. Ashley was holding it in her hand in the kitchen, while Greg was playing in his playroom down the hall. She put the crystal down for less than a minute and when she went to pick it up, it was gone. When she went to check on Greg in the playroom, he had the crystal in his hand. Stunned, Ashley asked her son where he picked up the stone. Greg replied that someone had given it to him, but he did not know who.

Strange events continued to occur in the household. One day, while Ashley was doing dishes in the kitchen, someone or some*thing* pushed her in the lower back, right in the exact location that would be easily accessible to a child.

Even though Ashley had a better understanding of possible causes of her son's drastic behavior, none were solutions to the problem; none would rid her house of the evil entity and leave her family in peace. Ashley had heard of priests who blessed family homes that were troubled by ghosts or possessions, so she contacted a minister to help her. The minister came to her house to hear the whole story of the unusual goings-on and to interview Ashley and meet Greg. He asked Ashley question upon question about herself, her family, and her lifestyle. He asked if she worshipped Satan and if she had taken her son to see a doctor. Since demonic possessions are rare cases, he wanted to rule out all other options.

Toward the end of their conversation and still skeptical, the minister was a few minutes away from leaving when all of a sudden, Greg went back into the trance-like state. The minister was able to see, right in front of him, what behavior Ashley was referring to. He sprayed Greg with holy water and he immediately recovered. This made a believer of the minister, and he said that he would return with a friend who was a highly sensitive person, almost a psychic. He also said that he believed that Greg was being possessed by a demon and that the demon was angry that Ashley let a man of God into her house. Before he left, the minister said a prayer and blessed the house.

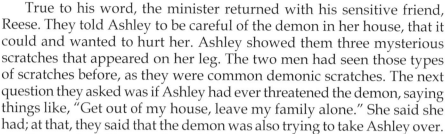

True to his word, the minister returned with his sensitive friend, Reese. They told Ashley to be careful of the demon in her house, that it could and wanted to hurt her. Ashley showed them three mysterious scratches that appeared on her leg. The two men had seen those types of scratches before, as they were common demonic scratches. The next question they asked was if Ashley had ever threatened the demon, saying things like, "Get out of my house, leave my family alone." She said she had; at that, they said that the demon was also trying to take Ashley over.

Reese asked Greg to show him his room. Greg pointed to an area of the room and Reese sensed a dark, hooded figure in the corner. The minister said that he would come back soon to thoroughly bless the house.

Between visits, more malevolent happenings took place. One afternoon, Ashley was trying to take a nap on the living room couch, but could not, due to the constant running and thumping she heard upstairs — when no one was actually up there. A while after, her mom witnessed a battery-less toy start and move.

Greg was still showing signs of possession. Every once in a while, his eyes would become glazed over and he would become belligerent in a trance. Since Reese and the minister sensed the presence of demons and spirits in the house, Ashley was wondering why her deceased grandmother, "Ma," was not putting an end to the demonic savagery bestowed upon her family. Truthfully, Ashley felt a bit mad at Ma for not helping out.

When the "demon-busting" team returned, the sensitive Reese answered some of Ashley's questions. Reese felt that a presence in the house was praying for the attacks to stop, but it was too big for them to handle. When Reese sketched a picture of the spirit he was communicating with, the sketch was of an older woman with gray hair and glasses that looked exactly like Ma. This made Ashley feel a little better that Ma was there, and was praying all she could, but the evil forces were too much. The minister said that once the house is blessed, it should get rid of the problem, but the length of time could vary greatly, from a couple of days to a couple of months. Ashley and her family were definitely hoping for the first choice.

While he was at the house, the minister also ran a voice recorder and could hear a voice distinctly saying "shut up" on it. Ashley's mother had a similar experience. She was talking on her cell phone to a friend and heard a voice say the same two words, "shut up," at a completely different time than the minister did. Ashley also heard the voice when she was on her cell phone with her best friend. All of the calls were made within the confines of the house. Also while the minister was there, he baptized both Ashley and Greg. He said that baptism worked as a demon repellent.

Soon after the blessing and the baptisms, the incidents ceased. The family was left alone in peace. Greg still sees spirits in the house and has reported one as a nice old man, which Ashley believes to be her grandfather who passed away while living there.

Although relieved that the haunting has stopped, Ashley and her family want answers to why this happened to them. In speaking with the family about the land surrounding their house, Ashley mentioned to the minister and Reese about the geology of their yard and woods. Reese had a friend who was an archeologist and was interested in seeing certain rocks that Ashley spoke of. About a quarter-mile into the woods behind their house, a path lead to an area of land with rocks sticking up in strange angles out of the ground. The archeologist immediately said that it looked as if that whole area was a Native American burial ground, possibly from the Mohegan tribe. He even saw quartz and granite rocks placed in that plot of land. The position of those rocks could indicate the importance of something that was buried underneath.

Ashley also told the archeologist that arrowheads were found nearby. He said that arrowheads were placed in burial grounds as tokens of remembrance. Arrowheads were rarely lost; instead, they were placed under headstones and other premeditated spots. Ashley's brother, Richard, had always thought that the place was a Native American burial ground and called it such when he was younger. Why demons though? Ashley did not practice Satanism, she did not fool around with a Ouija board, and Greg was too young to do or understand either. The investigative team asked if the stones had ever been tampered with. The whole area of the backyard could be a burial site, with marked and unmarked graves. One speculation for the "madness" could be that the fire pit that was built at the edge of the woods contained rocks that were actually grave markers. Another speculation was that one of Richard's friends, years earlier, lifted a few of the large rocks out of the speculative burial ground.

In one of the final conversations with the investigative team, they were able to answer a few more of Ashley's questions. When Ashley told the team about the Wiccan crystals and sage and the idea of the spirit of the little boy from down the street, they discredited those beliefs and practices. They said the Wiccan practices only made matters worse; just like the presence of the minister, those practices angered the demon further. They also stated that a demon can take on any shape, including that of a little child. Demons are Satan's helpers and are powerful. The reasoning behind the manifestation into a child-like entity was to lure Greg into playing with it. Ashley also expressed feelings of being watched and rooms seeming cloudy to her during the time of the haunting. Lastly, the minister also said that this has not been the only case of possession in Bozrah that he has been called to investigate.

Could this part of Bozrah be situated on holy ground? Recently a family of three boys and a single father had an incident where the father seemed to be possessed so horrifically that one boy attempted suicide to escape the anguish.

The archeologists will need to do more work in Ashley's backyard to figure out how extensive the ancient burial ground is underneath their property. Luckily for Ashley, Greg, and her family, their house and Greg are rid of any malevolent demonic encounters now.

However, even though Greg's demonic possession has been alleviated, ghosts are still seen within the household. Greg has become friends with the ghost he calls Ralph, who has taken residence in the house.

On one occasion, Ashley's mother came home from work and turned her bedroom light on, as a ghost walked through her and stood near the bedroom window. Ashley hears banging as a regular occurrence. Even though the demons seem to be cleared from the house, paranormal activity is constantly happening.

11.
Jewett City Vampires
Location: Griswold

Before the era of modern medicine and science, strange occurrences and tragedies were often credited to the supernatural. A bad crop season could have happened because the gods were offended in some way. Even in a Christian society, the devil was said to tempt good Christians, causing them to sin. Calamities befell individuals or a society either as a test from God or as punishment for their past indiscretions.

One of the most horrendous diseases of the nineteenth century was tuberculosis, or, as it was commonly known then, consumption. Consumption was the leading cause of death from the nineteenth century into the twentieth. Tuberculosis runs a course which "consumes" the body and leaves it wasting away. Symptoms include an incredible fever, mucus and bloody discharge, and the person's hue changing to a ghostlike white. Unfortunately, the result, more often than not in this time period, was death—a painful, slow death. Worse than that was the fact that tuberculosis was highly contagious and could wipe out whole families.

This leads to the story of the Jewett City's Ray family. Jewett City is the main hamlet in the town of Griswold. Henry Baker Ray and his wife had five children and some of their children had families of their own. In 1845, the seemingly healthy son of Henry Baker, Lemuel, was stricken with a disease that wasted him away and eventually claimed his life. Four years later, the father, Henry Baker Ray, came down with the same symptoms as Lemuel and also ended up perishing. Lemuel's brother, Elisha, passed away due to the same malady two years after his father. In 1854, another brother, Henry Nelson Ray, started having similar symptoms as the other three. The remaining Rays had had enough of this! This disease, or whatever it really was, was wiping out their whole family! The family suspected that there was more going on beneath the surface than solely consumption. They deduced that the deceased family members were returning from the dead and feasting on poor Henry Nelson. He was being "eaten alive" by more than just the disease.

The rest of the family decided to take matters into their own hands— literally. They used shovels and dug up the other two brothers (patriarchal respect must have made them leave Daddy alone) and burned their bodies right there in the graveyard. This way they would not be coming back for any more midnight feasts on Henry Nelson or any other family member.

Their vampire extermination methods did not fully work, though. Soon after, Henry Nelson was the next Ray to go, as he also died of consumption. The two remaining siblings did escape the jaws of disease and gruesome work of their brothers. Was it because of the cremation of their brothers' bodies, was it luck, or a bit of both? Henry Nelson's immediate family did not fare as well. Three of Henry Nelson's children also contracted tuberculosis and died. Speculation was that they were actually the meals of their father and other relatives.

The Ray family was not alone in the practice of desecrating the graves of suspected vampires to protect remaining family members' lives. Not far over the Rhode Island border from Jewett City, there were approximately five other cases, including three solely in the town of Exeter. What may sound morbid to our society today, full of scientific and medical knowledge, was a semi-commonplace practice used to rid the village of those nasty pests: vampires. Practices like rearranging the deceased culprits' bones, burning their vital organs, or in this case, whole bodies, were considered valid ways of protecting family members against the savagery of vampirism. Without the factual information of today, rural, superstitious societies came to their own conclusions of why such tragedies transpired.

It took me a while to find the stones of the Ray Family in the Jewett City Cemetery because they are not all located together, and the cemetery was slightly overgrown at the time of my visit.

The graves of the Ray family can be seen at the Jewett City Cemetery, located on Main Street, just off Route 12. The graves of Lemuel, Elisha, and Henry Baker Ray are located in the older part of the cemetery, closer to the back, while the grave of Henry Nelson is towards the front in the newer section.

While You're There:

Buttonwood Farm

All of that vampire hunting sure works up an appetite. Good thing that Griswold is home to one of the tastiest ice cream stands around. Buttonwood Farm, located at 473 Shetucket Turnpike, about a ten-minute drive from Jewett City, has homemade, deliciously creamy treats with flavors that include Forbidden Silk Chocolate, Peanut Butter, and Purple Cow. The farm also harvests huge fields of gorgeous sunflowers for sale by the bunch once a year for a small fee, which goes entirely to the Make-A-Wish Foundation. Before the harvest, this section of Connecticut resembles the French countryside with all of the sunflowers in bloom. In the fall, Buttonwood is home to hayrides and a corn maze.

12.
Creatures of the Woodland
Location: Franklin

Oftentimes, rural towns are home to a story or two. Whether it is a haunting, reputed cult practice, extraterrestrials, or other unusual oddities, in smaller, heavily wooded communities, tales and lore spread rapidly.

The Horse Creature

Franklin is a small town in the eastern part of the state comprised of mostly farm and woodland, where the cows outnumber the people. The most vivid story from Franklin comes from a gentleman named Jim, a lifelong Franklin resident. When Jim was younger, one of the jobs that he held was as a helper on a local farm. He worked there with his twin brother, doing odds and ends around the house and farmyard. The farm was relatively little, with small barnyard animals like pigs and sheep. One of Jim's jobs was to feed the animals. One day, while Jim and his brother were working, they noticed that the pigs had gotten out of their pen. The two brothers decided the best way to locate the missing swine was to split up. Jim chose a seldom-used trail that led from the farmyard to the adjacent woodlands. He was searching for the pigs to no avail, when something startled him. He looked up and saw off in the distance a "huge, white, dashing thing," which Jim describes as being horse-like, but much larger than an average-sized horse; this creature was seven to eight feet tall. Jim said that although the beast resembled a horse, it most emphatically was not one. There were no horses at this farm, and the closest horse stable was miles away (and a steady uphill mountain climb).The monster was standing, but its head and torso were making erratic movements, almost as if it were bucking.

Understandably, Jim ran back to the house frightened. He felt he needed to explain the last few minutes' events to the farmers so that they could tell him that he was dreaming and to snap out of it. Instead, they reacted differently. It seemed that they were not surprised to hear what Jim encountered. Even fifteen years later, Jim has vivid mental images of what he saw on that unforgettable day at work.

Red Eye

Not only does Franklin have its horse creature, but it also has a mysterious figure known as Red Eye that lurks in the woods of Ayer Mountain. Not much is known except that it is a monster that skulks in the woods, right off of Route 207 in Franklin.

Both Franklin tales come from the area where Route 32 meets Route 207.

While You're There:

Blue Slope Farm and Country Museum

Another unique Franklin destination is the Blue Slope Farm and Country Museum. Visitors are welcome to witness a real live working farm that also showcases tools and other historical artifacts that were used in the early years of the United States. Horse-drawn wagon and sleigh rides are also available seasonally. The Blue Slope Farm has cows, horses, rabbits, and other animals that the whole family can enjoy.

The museum is open by appointment, so first call ahead at 860-642-6413.

13.
Classic
Connecticut Folklore
Locations: Canton and Meriden

Two classic components of folklore and mythology have incarnations in the Nutmeg State: the headless horseman and the hell hound.

The Headless Horseman

Connecticut's headless horseman is based on a tale of a French paymaster who spent a fateful night in the fall of 1777 at the Horsford Tavern in Canton on the Hartford-Albany Road en route to pay French soldiers in Saratoga, New York. He arrived at the tavern on horseback, with saddle bags full of silver and gold. After spending the evening in the company of the locals, the Frenchman slumbered in one of the boarding rooms in the upstairs of the tavern.

The evening in the tavern was the last that anyone saw of him. When asked, the tavern keeper said that the paymaster left the next morning on his way to fulfill his instructions. When it was clear that the Frenchman was never going to arrive in Saratoga, suspicion abounded in the town of Canton, although there was no substantial evidence to convict anyone, not even the insalubrious tavern proprietor. Eventually, talk died down in town, and the French paymaster was nearly forgotten about.

Fast-forward about a hundred years when the Horsford Tavern met an untimely demise, burning to the ground. Among the smoking embers of the establishment, embedded in the base of the building, a headless skeleton was found. Soon after this grisly discovery was made, the townspeople's fear became reality; the tavern keeper had killed the paymaster!

Soon after the discovery, the Frenchman literally galloped back into the lives of Canton's residents. Startled witnesses in town started seeing a phantom horseman, riding west on the Hartford-Albany Road mounted on a ghostly steed with fiery eyes. Even today, the story of Canton's headless rider still permeates through the region. Drivers on today's Route 44 have witnessed the beheaded paymaster's journey west to Saratoga. Motorists have swerved off the road in fear of colliding with the phantasmal rider and his spectral horse.

Just like in the time of his demise, the phantom's route is a major thoroughfare, linking Hartford with western Connecticut, although in modern times the Hartford-Albany Turnpike is littered with Italian restaurants, car dealerships, and fast-food joints, instead of the Horsford Tavern.

Beware, if you are heading west down the old Hartford-Albany Turnpike, there may be something worse than the annoying SUV tailing you in the rearview. On trips down Route 44, I have yet to see the headless rider, but I am still looking!

The Black Dog

Since ancient mythology, the hell hound has been the subject of a commonly told tale among civilizations and cultures of the world. In more modern times, a supernatural black dog has been associated with the devil throughout Europe and most prominently in England.

Although a cute, dark Spaniel with a wagging tail does not conjure up the same kind of ferocious images as a fire-breathing hound of hell, Connecticut's cute harbinger of misery has at least six deaths attributed to it. Located up on the West Peak of the Hanging Hills in Meriden, this little beast has quite the omen surrounding it. The story goes that the first time one sees the dog it shall bring them joy, the second time sorrow, and the third, well, death.

The Hanging Hills are low-altitude mountains closer to the sea than most. The Hills are full of neat geologic features and are a favorite of mountain climbers. The most infamous report of the Black Dog came from a geologist who was visiting the Hanging Hills from New York. His name was W.H.C. Pynchon. In February 1891, Pynchon and a friend named Herbert Marshall were researching the geology of the Hanging Hills when they spotted the dog.

Earlier, while conversing with one another, Pynchon told Marshall of a small dog that he had seen while visiting The Hills once before. The dog followed Pynchon for much of his hike. Odd, Pynchon noted, though, was the silent bark emitted from the happy little guy. Marshall stated that he too had seen the dog on two previous visits to the Hanging Hills.

Soon after the two men saw the dog, Marshall's foot slipped on ice and he plummeted to his death, falling off the mountain. The third visit from the dog was the end of Marshall and the second for Pynchon and caused him great sorrow, just as the legend told.

In reading Pynchon's account, he even mentions that a Harvard educated man of science, like himself, should not believe such poppycock as a cursed dog. W.H.C. Pynchon had written his account in the *Connecticut Quarterly*.

A little while later, Pynchon decided to do more research in Tthe Hills and retrace the steps that he and his ill-fated friend took earlier. Sadly, Pynchon was never able to relate the details of this trip to Meriden, since near the same location that Marshall perished, Pynchon too was accidentally killed. The Curse of the Black Dog was at work again!

In his article from the *Connecticut Quarterly*, Pynchon prophesied his own annihilation at the paws of the black dog.

The latest incident of the curse of the black dog happened on Thanksgiving Day in 1972 when a hiker fell to his death.

On my trip to the Hanging Hills, the only black dogs I saw were on leashes in Hubbard Park, a Frederick Law Olmstead-designed town park, located at the foot of East and West Peak.

Hubbard Park has amenities such as picnic areas, a pond, a pool, and a performance space. Hikers can venture up the mountainsides in a series of trails. A paved car road takes the visitor up the mountains past West Peak, terminating on the top of East Peak, which is capped off by a stone tower called Castle Craig. On a clear day, the sightseer can see the Berkshires of Massachusetts to the northwest and Long Island Sound to the south.

14.
Melon Heads
Locations: Fairfield and many towns between New Haven and Bridgeport

Sightings of Melon Heads, a group of inbred "people" living in the woods, is not just specific to Connecticut, but variations of the story are also found in the Midwest, Ohio, and Michigan. Connecticut has slightly different versions of the Melon Head legend, with two of the most abundant sightings being centered around the towns of Shelton and Trumbull. Many other towns, mainly in Fairfield County, have had Melon Head sightings as well.

Fairfield Melon Heads

This particular adaptation comes from the town of Fairfield.

A band of Melon Heads are said to live in the woods behind Lake Mohegan, a popular family spot for hiking and swimming. The version, similar to other variations, depicts the Melon Heads as human beings with large, bulbous heads and globular, bulging eyes. The Melon Heads have lived in the woods for years and the reason they look so abnormal is due to excessive inbreeding.

Lake Baby

If the Melon Heads are not reason enough to visit Lake Mohegan, there are more legends associated with this spot. Supposedly, a baby was buried at the bottom of the lake.

Other Variations of the Melon Heads

In other locations, the Melon Heads are presented as mean. Some people say that the Melon Heads have been seen, albeit rarely, out in public at places like the grocery store. One variation is that a mental hospital burned down and patients have lived in the woods for years. Another includes the Melon Heads as victims of a crazy scientist who performed experiments on them, and yet another presents them as a family accused of witchcraft, who have been in hiding since in the 1800s.

So-called "Dracula Drive," actually named Velvet Street in Trumbull, and in Shelton, Saw Mill City Road, are supposed Melon Head roads.

Whoever the Melon Heads are, whether a group of inbred humans, some kind of alien life forms, or the product of local tall tales spun by high school students, they are more than a little prevalent in southern and southwestern Connecticut.

So if you happen to be hiking the trails of Lake Mohegan and see someone, or some*thing*, with a humongous, spherical head, you have most likely run into one of Connecticut's legendary Melon Heads!

Lake Mohegan is located off of Exit 46 on the Merritt Parkway, on 960 Morehouse Highway in Fairfield.

While You're There:

Senor Salsa

If the thought of large-headed beings make you work up an appetite, stop off at Senor Salsa on Route 1 in Fairfield, before you head up Interstate 95. Senor Salsa, until recently part of the west coast "La Salsa" Mexican food chain, serves great quesadillas, tacos, and burritos, with quick service! The best part of Senor Salsa is, hence the name, their salsas. Customers can choose from a substantial array of mild, medium, and spicy salsas to accompany their quesadillas. As you wait for your meal to be made, help yourself to filling small plastic containers with the spicy goodness.

Even scarier than the Melon Heads, though, is Senor Salsa's parking lot during a peak meal time; don't say you haven't been warned!

15.
Gardner Lake
Locations: Salem, Montville

Most Connecticut residents know Gardner Lake as a popular vacation rental spot, with swimming, fishing, boating, and all kinds of other water activities.

In the late nineteenth century, a man named Thomas LeCount wanted to move his house from one side of the lake to the other side of the lake. The most logical time to move an entire house across the middle of the lake would be in winter, when the ice is thick and the house could be transported somewhat easily by a team of draft animals.

The move was taking more time than originally allotted and night was coming in, so the crew decided to finish the job at first light. They arrived the next day only to find that ice was cracking and the house was about to fall into the lake! Only when the ice entirely thawed in the springtime did the house become almost fully submerged. For years after, the top of the house was still seen emerging from the water, but eventually it became fully waterlogged and sank to the bottom. Legend goes that on certain nights, soft sounds of piano music can be heard by visitors to Gardner Lake. Fishermen report that to this day, be it mermaids, phantoms, or walleye, the sunken piano still plays.

While You're There:

Salem Apple Festival

A yearly tradition at the Congregational Church in Salem is the Salem Apple Festival. This small event attracts hundreds of hungry visitors annually. At the festival, visitors can sample fine apple fare like fritters, pie, and apple crisp. It takes place on a Saturday at the end of October. Also on display are local crafts and demonstrations by civic groups. The event is free; just expect long lines, especially for the apple fritters!

The Salem Apple Festival is located in the center of town on Route 85, not very far from Gardner Lake.

Annual Salem Book Sale

Also happening in town at the same time is the annual Salem book sale. There will be at least something for everyone at this book fair that fills up a school gymnasium.

The book fair takes place at Salem Elementary School, which is located a little farther south on Route 85.

16.
Maud's Grave
Location: Sterling

Nestled in a heavily wooded section of eastern Connecticut is the town of Sterling. Pachaug State Forest, which is the largest forest in Connecticut, comprises much of the towns of Voluntown, Sterling, and Griswold. This particular legend comes directly from those very woods. The story is one of the most well-known legends in this part of the state, and, depending on who is telling the story, varies greatly. Growing up in Eastern Connecticut, the story of Maud was commonly heard. The first version of the tale is what I was told growing up and the ones that follow are variations I have heard since.

Although the exact location of Maud's grave is disputed, all the supposed locations of Maud's Grave are situated near the aptly named "Hell Hollow Road" in Sterling. In the time before hospitals and doctor's offices were accessible to all, some villagers took matters into their own hands with herbal remedies to cure the townspeople's maladies.

Maud was one such villager, concocting potions to heal the sick. She was an older woman who lived alone and helped and cured many people. One day, though, a boy who was suffering from an undisclosed illness was given a home remedy from Maud. Sadly, the boy did not survive. Even though Maud had helped many others in Pachaug Village, Maud was labeled as a "witch" and was buried alive. The reasoning was that since she was a witch, she would be able to fly out of the filled hole. Unfortunately for her, she was not able to soar out and perished by suffocation.

Ever since, strange occurrences have started happening in this section of the forest. Even though the village of Pachaug has long since been abandoned, traces of Maud and the village still exist today. There were stories of cars shutting down or not being able to start on Hell Hollow Road. In the 1970s, on Halloween night, four friends were to meet on Hell Hollow Road, near the pond at midnight. Two of the boys got there first and poured a strip of gasoline on the road. As they saw their friends' truck coming around the corner, they lit the strip with a match and the road quickly became a wall of flame. Their friends turned right around and never returned.

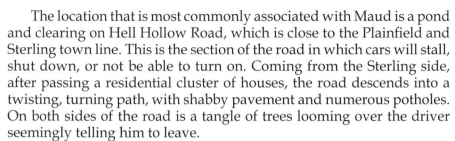

The location that is most commonly associated with Maud is a pond and clearing on Hell Hollow Road, which is close to the Plainfield and Sterling town line. This is the section of the road in which cars will stall, shut down, or not be able to turn on. Coming from the Sterling side, after passing a residential cluster of houses, the road descends into a twisting, turning path, with shabby pavement and numerous potholes. On both sides of the road is a tangle of trees looming over the driver seemingly telling him to leave.

After further research, the location of Maud's Grave seems to not actually be on Hell Hollow Road, but across Route 49, on Cedar Swamp Road. Located about a half-mile from the intersection with Route 49, the traveler will pass a cemetery on the right side. A few yards after, a path will cross the road. The entrance to this location of Maud's Grave is down the path to the right. Walking this trail a few minutes will bring the visitor to a location of old foundations and stone walls. This is the supposed location of Maud's Grave. Orbs have been seen floating around the foundations and Maud's Grave is reportedly located here, broken into parts.

In other variations of the tale of Maud, she is the ghost of a little girl who died while a young child. Other stories from this section of Pachaug include a ghost of a colonial soldier on the street, unusual objects being seen, and the howls of a Native American woman who was massacred by soldiers near the pond off Hell Hollow Road.

My experiences with Maud's Grave were semi-fruitful. While growing up, a trip up Hell Hollow Road was the place to go to flat-out scare ourselves. One Halloween, a group of friends decided to go to the location of Maud's Grave, or where we originally thought it was located, on the path around the pond on Hell Hollow. While a few of us started down the path, three of us who had not reached it yet saw a white light shining like a spotlight, protruding from the woods or from the sky. Soon it was gone; upon further investigation, no one could tell where the light had come from. We drove past the area, and along Route 49, trying to catch another glimpse, but had no luck.

Was it a searchlight of some kind? Possibly, but the desolate woods of Sterling is a strange place to put such a light. Many years later, after finding out the other location where the grave could be, another group went to search for it. On a humid, mosquito-filled day in July, we ventured off Cedar Swamp Road to find Maud's Grave and the foundations. After a few minutes walking down the path, we came across the foundations, but no sign of the grave. We ventured further down the path for about fifteen more minutes, but still could not locate it.

Returning to the area of the foundations, we searched for the headstone, but found nothing. I snapped a few pictures of the foundation area as well as a broken stone that looked similar to the headstone of Maud.

Even though we did not feel, see, or experience anything unusual in the woods, other than being covered by mosquito bites, one photo did show a white orb hovering over a foundation. There was no rain in sight that day, so the possibility that the object in the photo was a raindrop is ruled out. After about an hour of searching, on the way out, we traveled every side path to make sure we did not miss the grave, but left without success.

Is the grave further destroyed? Was it the multiple broken stone that we saw? Does the grave exist on Hell Hollow and not off Cedar Swamp Road? We will never know for certain, but in any case, Hell Hollow Road and Maud's Grave do provide the visitor with an un-peaceful, eerie feeling!

One of the possible locales of Maud's Grave. What exactly is that object in the middle of the picture? (Note: there was NO precipitation the day the photo was taken.)

While You're There:

Ekonk Hill Turkey Farm

Visit the Ekonk Hill Turkey Farm in Sterling. Although called a turkey farm, the name can be misleading. Ekonk Hill features some of the tastiest ice cream in the area. The bucolic setting is perfect for a mid-afternoon rest and cone. The farm, true to its name, does feature live turkeys and take-home turkey delicacies.

The Ekonk Hill Turkey Farm is located on Route 49 North (Ekonk Hill Road) in Sterling.

17.
Tales of Old Brooklyn
Location: Brooklyn

Tucked away on a back road, in the sleepy town of Brooklyn, lies a small wooden church. Unlike many older churches that are located in town or village centers, this church is off the beaten path. It is small by comparison to other New England colonial parish churches, but certainly does not lack character. It has a wooden frame and is built in a style more typical of a house, rather than a traditional church with a protruding steeple.

Trinity Church was built in 1771 by Godfrey Malbone, who moved from Newport, Rhode Island, to Brooklyn. The church is actually a replica of Touro Synagogue, which is America's oldest synagogue and still stands in Newport today. Surrounding the church on all sides is a revolutionary-era cemetery. The trees behind the church are planted in a cruciform shape. The second floor of the church was where the slaves attended mass when accompanying their masters to service. Carved names of slaves can still be seen in the walls of the upper level.

Old Trinity Church in Brooklyn has its share of ghostly and grisly associations. Whether fact or fiction, the church presents an eerie aura.

For the most part, Church Street is a modern road with houses and abutting developments, on the aptly named Malbone Lane. Trinity is located about half a mile from the intersection with Route 6. It is shaded under a grove of cross-shaped trees, with the ancient burying stones swarming around its wooden sides. Adding to the eerie feeling are the "No Trespassing" signs that are littered among the trees. One may question the use of signs like these on an active church, but this church does come with a bit of a reputation.

A Serial Killer's Dump Site

Michael Ross, a serial killer who preyed on female victims in Eastern Connecticut in the early '80s, some say discarded the bodies of his first Connecticut victims behind this church. Further legend says that he even wrote messages with their blood on the back wall of the church. In reality, Ross dumped the first Connecticut victim on this road, but not actually on the church property. Couple the Ross stories with sightings of Satan worshippers and psychic mediums who have felt possessed here, and the notoriety of the location grows.

An Important Horse

To some, Trinity Church is an idyllic country parish, with charm and panache, whereas to others, it is a foreboding place of intrigue and mystery. The church is still used by the parish on occasion, but the newer, more majestic location of Trinity Church, referred to as "New Trinity," is located in the town center, where Routes 6 and 169 meet. This church, common to most other Episcopal churches in New England, is made of stone. Trinity is unique because it has two Tiffany windows. Louis Comfort Tiffany, famous for his work in glass, was the son of Charles Tiffany, the founder of what would be known as Tiffany and Co. Charles lived in Brooklyn before he started the jewelry company in New York City.

The church builder, Godfrey Malbone, was a Tory; he swore allegiance to the crown and did not believe in the Colonies' separation from England. Godfrey had many African slaves. One of his slaves had a son named Rufus. Often slaves took the surname of the family he or she worked for, so his name was Rufus Malbone. Rufus became a well-known freed slave who lived up the road on the Putnam-Pomfret border. Rufus had a horse named Dolly that often pulled his cart through the roads of northeastern Connecticut as he bought and sold produce.

Rufus, so enamored of this horse, asked with his dying wish, that Dolly be buried beside him in his grave. Once Rufus passed on, Dolly became unruly and wild. The neighbors convened and it was decided that the horse had to be put down. In the wake of Dolly's death, the neighbors followed Rufus's instructions. They opened the grave that Rufus lay in and placed the body of his trusting horse next to him.

A Wolf Massacre

Brooklyn's most famous native son was the military hero Israel Putnam. Putnam fought in battles in Montreal, at Bunker Hill, and at Ticonderoga, New York. He escaped death numerous times. Like a cat, Putnam seemed to have nine lives. He was once almost burned at the stake by a Native American tribe; he survived a shipwreck in Cuba; and he escaped from being captured in Quebec and made his way back to Southern New England through the woods of Vermont. In addition to being an unprecedented military man in both the French and Indian War and the American Revolution, in December 1792, "Old Putt" was said to have killed the last wolf in Connecticut.

Today, the location of the killing occurring at the wolf den can be seen up the road in Pomfret, at Mashmoquet State Forest, where the visitor can take the Wolf Den Trail to see the site of Putnam's famous wolf massacre. There is a statue located in front of the Brooklyn Historical Society of Israel on horseback. On either side of the rather large pedestal that supports the Putnam statue are two wolf heads. The original bronze wolf heads were stolen by a Brooklyn Fair carnival worker traveling through town years ago. The heads have been restored and this time are immovable!

While You're There:

Today, Brooklyn is still home to the country's longest-running country fair. The center of town is located off of Exit 91 off Interstate 395. Visitors can see the statue of Putnam and the outside of both Trinity churches. Another of Brooklyn's quirky features is the Creamery Brook Bison Farm, located on Purvis Road. Visible from the road is a grazing herd of bison, not a typical sight in New England. The public is also allowed to tour the farm and buy bison products in the store.

18.
The Poor Farm and Alms House
Location: Norwich

This marker nea Norwich's prese day Pawsitive D Park is a memor to the numerous unmarked bodie laid to rest underneath the ground.

In the years before state institutions became commonplace, towns used poor farms, asylums, or alms houses to care for their destitute, cognitively delayed, or mentally ill. Norwich was no exception. Norwich's alms house was located on Asylum Street, on the site where now Pawsitive Park is located—the local dog park. Tragedy struck the Norwich Alms House on the night of March 12, 1876. A fire broke out in the building. The mentally unstable were housed on the third floor in locked rooms. Horrendously, they burned to death before the fire department could arrive. At that time, this poor farm was located a good distance from the downtown, before the existence of automobile/fire engines, alarm systems, or fire escapes. The fire department did not get word of the blaze right away and by the time they arrived, the heat of the blaze was too strong and sixteen people tragically perished. Onlookers who gathered at the site recalled that they heard pounding on the walls and windows and could hear dreadful screams of the dying. By the time the fire was snuffed out, only a brick façade was left standing; the interior was completely gutted.

When they died, both residents and the sixteen from the fire, who did not have friends or family, were buried in a potter's field adjacent to the Alms House until the mid-1920s. The bodies of the destitute and disabled were buried anonymously in this lot. The number varies from over 100 to 212 unmarked graves.

After the fire of 1876, the asylum was rebuilt. It was used for many years until it was replaced by the more modern Norwich State Hospital. When its use was discontinued, it lay abandoned and eventually caught fire again, destroying most of the structure in 1956.

Today, a monument exists next to the dog park with a memorial to the 212 nameless bodies that decompose beneath the grounds. A basement or foundation level exists on the abutting Alms House Road. Now the rooms are often illegally used by homeless squatters. How ironic that in a way, it still serves its early purpose.

According to legend, a nurse carrying medical bags has been seen floating about the property. The most common sights, though, are tail-wagging pooches enjoying a romp any day of the year.

The former asylum was located at the corner of Alms House Road and Asylum Street in Norwich.

Section 3
Off-Kilter
Places

A giant Easter Island statue greets visitors to the Timexpo Museum in Waterbury

1.
The Blue Lady
Location: Norwich

Located on Lafayette Street in Norwich, the Yantic Cemetery is a testament to the past wealth of the city in the late nineteenth and early twentieth centuries. The immensity of some of the family stones in this dead city is tangible evidence of Norwich's affluent and storied past. Tombstones of note include that of Lafayette Foster, a monument to Norwich's fallen heroes of the Civil War, and the Osgood Memorial. The cemetery even includes a tribute to Norwich's heroes who died at Andersonville, the notorious Confederate prison camp.

Sarah Larned's grave was marked by the statue of the Blue Lady until it was vandalized in 2010. The statue was known to evoke a sudden feeling of forlornness in the visitor.

Cemeteries undoubtedly herald the most supernatural stories. Many cemeteries that do not have a known legend associated with them simply *feel* eerie. The Yantic Cemetery is certainly one of these. Norwich, in the nineteenth century, was one of the most prosperous towns in the country, with its economy based on the numerous textile mills dotting the three rivers in the town. It was home to notable figures such as Lafayette Foster, the acting vice president under Andrew Johnson, and Smith and Wesson of the firearms fame.

Located on Lafayette Street, this cemetery, which permanently houses the remains of former Norwich aristocrats, contains monuments that reach twenty feet or higher. One of the largest, located in the far end of the cemetery, is a high-rise obelisk commemorating the lives of the Osgood family. Charles Osgood was the mayor of Norwich during a time when the city flourished. Although this structure is impressive in itself, it pales in comparison to the statue that once sat below it. Crouched over the tomb of Sarah Larned Osgood was a life-size replica of a woman, possibly the Virgin Mary, aptly nicknamed "The Blue Lady." Made of bronze and wearing a blue gown, she has remained in the same location for more than 119 years, bowing on top of the placard bearing Mrs. Osgood's name, looking lifelike amidst the city of graves in the

Yantic Cemetery. One would swear that her eyes were real and not metal, especially when basked in the glow of car headlights. There was speculation that this statue was the work of famed sculptor Augustus Saint-Gaudens, although it was later found to be untrue.

Although there was no specific story attributed to The Blue Lady, she was worth a look, a stare, and a mention. Sadly, this story has to be written in the past tense. In 2010, The Blue Lady was savagely stolen from her resting place of almost 120 years. Chunks of the statue turned up at a scrap yard, except for the head, later to be found perched atop a wall in a vacant lot in Willimantic. The town hopes to restore the statue, but nothing is for certain. The perpetrators were later caught and arrested.

In fall 2011, the story of the tragic tale of The Blue Lady received a happy ending. The pieces were all recovered; the head thief will spend time behind bars; and Norwich's City Council passed legislation that approved the statue to be refurbished, so that it might once again be hunched over the grave of Sarah Larned Osgood.

This cemetery is located on Lafayette Street in Norwich, right next to the Backus Hospital.

2.
The Crypt of the Center Church-on-the-Green
Location: New Haven

When researching the "other side" of Connecticut travel and history, researchers tend to spend time exploring cemeteries. Why is the cemetery that is affiliated with New Haven's Center Church-on-the-Green so different then? Well for one, it is inside. Yes, when the Center Church (which in spite of the name is located on the edge of picturesque New Haven Green) was built, it was erected on top of a portion of the New Haven Cemetery. When it was constructed, between the years of 1812 and 1814, it was built raised so that it could literally be above this section of the New Haven burial ground without disturbing the stones and inhabitants underneath. The crypt is a prime example of an ancient colonial New England burial ground.

The years of the under-church interments were from 1687 to 1812. The visitor can see images such as death heads on the stones representing sickness and sadness to warn the onlooker that life can be miserable and to provide an active reminder of death.

Stones from this period coincide with the religion of New England residents of the day, Puritanism. Extremely devout and pious, the death's head grave symbol exemplified the religious thought of the Puritans. This was also a time that death was a prominent part of life, with disease running rampant and infant mortality rates very high. In general, the gravestone etchings of New England tend to be representative of the general society. (For a detailed contrast, compare the stones of Norwich's Ancient Burying Ground on East Town Street to Yantic Cemetery, also in Norwich, to reference the stylistic differences between early eighteenth and nineteenth century gravestones.) The oldest stone in the crypt has the death's head depiction on it. The stone is that of Sarah Rutherford Trowbridge. Benedict Arnold's first wife, Margaret Mansfield, is also buried here.

In addition to the common headstone-style gravestone, this cemetery also boasts tomb tables (gravestones that are made of stone and are shaped like a table), wolf tables (another table-style marker, used so that wolves or other animals did not dig up the bodies), and sundials. Inscriptions on the stones reflect sentiments echoed by the Puritan religion of the day, with warnings like, "My time has come, your time will come too, use your time for the glory of God," serving as directives to visitors both past and present.

New Haven's Center-Church-on-the-Green was built on top of an old burial ground. Presently, the cemetery is located in the church's basement.

The scariest part of the crypt and tour is the low ceilings. If you are over six feet, duck! My traveling companion had to spend the whole tour hunched over, so as not to be constantly hitting his head. The stones range from gray to reddish-brown. The floor is inlayed with brick and the stones are surrounded by sand. The New Haven Crypt Association has done extensive work in preserving the stones. With moisture, the sandstone graves eventually become sand, so the Association has taken measures to battle against Mother Nature and safeguard the stones. This includes preserving the base of the stones with lead. Even though they have preserved many, they still have more to go. In general, though, the Center Church crypt is a great way to see colonial New England gravestones that have been mostly untouched by the elements or vandalism. Unlike many churchyards or old burial grounds where stones may be broken, weathered with time, or neglected, this church basement holds true remnants of the past on view in the present.

Outside, the church borders the New Haven Green. This center of town is known for family picnics, concerts, and generally, people enjoying themselves outside on nice days. The revelers on the Green are actually reveling on the remains of 5,000 unnamed former New Havenites. What is now the town green, was the original city burial ground. When the Grove Street Cemetery opened, the headstones were moved from the green to it, but the bodies were not. So the ancient stones in the cemetery do not have corresponding bodies. The cemetery underneath Center Church was originally part of that cemetery and is the only section that remains intact, although now covered by the church.

Today, tour guides of Center Church show visitors not only the crypt, but the inside of the church as well, including a beautiful Tiffany window.

To see this cemetery for yourself, visit the Center Church-on-the-Green during the months from April to November, on a Thursday or a Saturday between 11 a.m. and 1 p.m. for a tour of the church and especially, the crypt. The Center Church-on-the-Green is located at 311 Temple Street in New Haven.

While You're There:

Frank Pepe Pizzeria and Sally's Apizza

A close second to the higher education of Yale, New Haven is best known for its pizza, and rightly so. With Frank Pepe Pizzeria and Sally's Apizza leading the way, New Haven's pizza is truly top-notch. The thin crust, arriving straight from the brick oven, is truly a taste treat. The white clam pizza at Pepe's is full of garlic and loaded with freshly shucked clams. It is made without red sauce and is an item that any seafood and pizza lover should try at least once.

Even though there are branches of Pepe's located throughout the state, the New Haven original is an experience. Be prepared to wait in lines though, as they do not take reservations. Make sure to check out The Spot, located next-door, to see if the line there is any shorter. Pepe's has a no-frills service, with a limited menu consisting of only pizza. Drinks include soda, water, wine, and beer. If you feel weak from a tour of the Center Church Crypt, an Apizza from Pepe's or Sally's will be just what you're looking for. Both Sally's and Pepe's are located on Wooster Street in New Haven.

3.
Slater Museum
Location: Norwich

Want to see a Michelangelo but are not able to get to Rome? Want to see the Winged Goddess of Victory, but cannot afford a trip to Paris? Do not fear. To see these and other masterpieces, just take a quick trip to Norwich's Slater Memorial Museum. The museum, located on the campus of Norwich Free Academy, is one of three art museums housed in a high school in the United States. The museum includes an extensive cast gallery with sculpture hailing from Ancient Greece and Rome to the Italian Renaissance. The museum was a gift to the school from William Slater, named for the memory of his father, John Fox Slater. Construction was started in 1886, and the building was dedicated in November of 1888. The building itself is most impressive. With a brick façade adorned with arches, chimneys, and slanted roofs, Slater is three stories tall and even includes a tower, which is said to be haunted....

The most eye-catching exhibit is the cast gallery, which is not an artist's rendering of original masterworks, but instead the originals were actually covered with a layer of plaster and casts were made. The cast gallery is housed in an impressive open-gallery area, highlighted by the Winged Victory or Nike of Samothrace. Along the edges of the center section are Greek figures from a pediment in the Temple of Zeus and a bas relief from the Parthenon. Outside the perimeter of the "Great Hall" is a rectangle full of master works, including *The Seated Boxer*, *The Wrestlers*, *Otricoli Zeus*, and *Venus de Milo*. Slater showcases much more than copies of statues though. This floor also contains Native American and African art and artifacts, work from the Hudson River School, and pieces from the local painter, John Denison Crocker.

On the floor overlooking the great hall is a delightful hodgepodge of art and artifacts. The collection varies widely, from eighteenth century American home furnishings and samurai armor to a vast collection of antique guns and a giant cast of Moses, as well as a cast of the Pieta. There are stairs leading to Slater Tower, but they are off limits due to safety concerns and, rumor has it, paranormal activity!

The back of Slater Memorial Museum is attached to Converse Art Gallery, built in 1901 and named after its benefactor. This exhibit hall features annual Connecticut artists' shows, student work, and various rotating exhibitions.

Norwich Free Academy's Slater Museum is home to an extensive cast gallery, as well as original art and artifacts.

The first floor of Slater is predominantly an auditorium used for school and community events. On either side of the stage are large portraits of NFA's founders. In previous years, the two stoic gentlemen's portraits were joined by about ten other solemn, unsmiling faces of NFA's original patrons. The most memorable was the man who was wearing an eye patch, which was flipped up to expose the eyeless socket. That portrait and the others are presently in storage.

Slater Museum is located on the campus of Norwich Free Academy at 305 Broadway in Norwich. Admission is $3 for adults and $2 for students and seniors. Enter Slater Memorial Museum through the newly built, very impressive glass atrium that connects four of the campus buildings. Take the elevator to the museum floor. Try to plan your visit at the time of the blooming cherry blossoms that line the walkways of NFA's beautiful college-like campus during the first weeks in May. Enjoy your visit, but do not be surprised if someone is watching you from atop the tower!

4.
Joseph Steward's Museum of Curiosities and the Old State House
Location: Hartford

The Charles Bulfinch-designed Old State House in Hartford attracts more than just history buffs to the *Hart-beat* of Connecticut. Although in the Old State House the visitor can look into historic courtrooms where the Amistad trial first took place and enjoy an interactive exhibit on the history of Hartford, the real draw to the Old State House is Joseph Steward's Museum of Curiosities. Heck, who wouldn't want to see a two-headed calf?

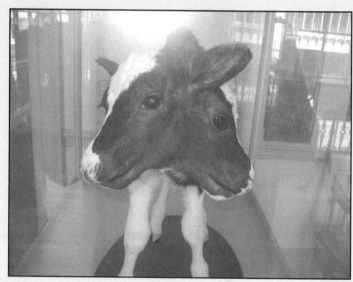

A stillborn two-headed calf on display at Joseph Steward Museum of Curiosities located in the Old State House in Hartford.

The Old State House, built in 1796, was used as the capitol building of Connecticut during years when the capital city alternated between Hartford and New Haven. The Old State House was active until 1873, when the beautiful, present-day, gold-domed capitol was built up the road right near Bushnell Park. The Connecticut colony was formed from combining the Hartford and New Haven colonies. This brick structure replaced the 1720 state house that had caught fire during celebrations declaring the end of the American Revolution. Written here were the Fundamental Orders of Connecticut, which became Connecticut's Constitution, thus the nickname "The Constitution State."

When entering the museum, first peer into the courtrooms and senate chambers and view the Statue of Justice. On this same floor, down the hall, is the Curiosities Museum. In a room that used to be the office of the Secretary of State, and prior to that served as a porch, lies a collection of miscellaneous odd objects in the natural history realm. Joseph Steward opened a museum of this kind in the attic of the Old State House in 1795, and it was one of America's first museums. In this re-creation, the visitor is first greeted on both sides of the room's entrance by many smiling animal heads, my favorite being the boar's head, which is literally smiling.

Another view into Joseph Steward Museum of Curiosities. The collection includes many stuffed animals, including mountain goats and an alligator hung upside down.

There is so much to look at and observe in this small room, close inspection is needed since with only a glance you will miss much. The highlight of the collection is the two-headed calf. Yes, it is a real two-headed calf, although it was stillborn. The calf is not the only two-headed item. There is also a two-headed pig. This piglet also died before being born and is now preserved in a liquid-filled jar. The calf and piglet were acquired in 1996. Mounted on the wall is the front half of a large mountain goat, feet and all. There are long snake skins, a turtle shell, a crocodile, and a puffer fish, as well. Stuffed birds line the right-hand wall. Not for the squeamish, the collection also includes a mummified human hand, and even worse for my traveling companion for this adventure, an assortment of mounted butterflies. Steward's museum is even home to a unicorn horn, which is actually a Narwhal tusk.

Although not "odd" per say, in the basement of the Old State House is an interactive exhibit chronicling the history of Hartford from the pre-colonial and colonial days through the present. Included are displays on former Hartford stalwart, the department store G. Fox, the road and highway system, and the gun manufacturing industry in town. Visitors are even allowed to dress up like their favorite Whaler: you can don the old green and white and pretend that you are Zarley Zalapski or Ron Francis.

Touching on the issue of the Whalers, another curious fact of Connecticut is that it seems the Hartford Whalers hockey team is more popular today than it was while it was active, given the plethora of hats, shirts, and other Whaler merchandise available for sale in and out of the state.

The Old State House is located in State Square. There is reasonably priced garage parking nearby.

While You're There:

Connecticut Whale & XL Center

Although the Whalers are no more, Hartford still has a minor league hockey team that plays in the American Hockey League. The Connecticut Whale provides family-friendly and affordable entertainment. The Whale play home games at the XL Center (formerly called the Hartford Civic Center) and pays homage to the city's former NHL team with a similar color scheme, fight song, and even Pucky the Whale, the beloved Whalers' mascot. The Whale is the farm team for the New York Rangers. Also in the AHL is the New York Islanders's affiliate, the Bridgeport Sound Tigers. Games are played from late fall through spring.

5.
Mental Health
Museum at the Institute of Living
Location: Hartford

Your Uncle Dave or Aunt Molly would have gone to a state hospital if they needed to dry out, be put on suicide watch, or just generally had a few screws loose. State institutions tended to resemble jails or haunted manors. Celebrities, such as Rodney Dangerfield, went to a more exclusive setting when they needed "time to themselves." Instead of Connecticut Valley Hospital, they spent time in the Institute of Living in Hartford. Although the Institute of Living was the first psychiatric hospital in the state, established in 1822, during the twentieth century it became known for housing the wealthy who needed a break from society.

Unlike most of the state hospitals, the Institute of Living is very much active. Today, it is affiliated with Hartford Hospital. Designed by one of the most lauded landscape architects ever, Fredrick Law Olmstead, this lovely estate is located behind a high brick wall. Although the Institute of Living provided a more comfortable and attractive setting than those provided by state hospitals, many of the same state mental health practices, such as lobotomies and electro-shock therapy, were implemented there as well.

Located at the back of the campus of the Institute is the Museum of Mental Health. The exhibit is entitled "Myths, Minds, and Medicine: Two Centuries of Mental Health Care." This small museum gives not only information on the history of the Institute, but of mental health care in general, including practices that were used in Hartford, even controversial ones. Among the reasons why patients were brought to Hartford, according to the museum, were "anxiety, substance abuse, depression, hallucinations, paranoia, and schizophrenia." There is a human brain housed in the museum, a display about drug therapy, as well as one on restraints, featuring a straitjacket. A section focuses on phrenology, which is the study of bumps on one's skull, based on a now discredited theory that the shape of the skull revealed personality traits. Photos of a lobotomy procedure and shock treatment for schizophrenia reveal the importance of these procedures in the mid-twentieth century. The museum also features displays on the lighter side of life at the hospital, such as photos of patients lounging around the pool.

The museum depicts the full spectrum of life at the hospital. It shows "shocking," sometimes gruesome, procedures used in the past juxtaposed with the humane, and for the time period, revolutionary treatments using the arts and recreation as therapy.

A trip to the Museum of Mental Health shows the visitor what a working mental health facility looks like today, especially in contrast to the abandoned state institutions of the same era. The small size of the museum gives the visitor a quick and convenient look into the history of the facility and of mental health practice. Hopefully Rodney Dangerfield was able to "get some respect" while at the Institute.

The museum is open from Monday through Friday, from 9 a.m. - 5 p.m. The Institute of Living is located at 200 Retreat Avenue.

While You're There:

Agave Grill

After all the talk of lobotomies and shock therapy, you must be hungry! Agave Grill is a perfect lunch spot. The Mexican restaurant features guacamole which is made at your table. The burritos and tacos are very flavorful and the restaurant has a comfortable, but elegant atmosphere. Agave Grill is located at 100 Allyn Street in Hartford.

6.

The Mysteries of Plum Island

Locations: The Lymes, Long Island Sound

Connecticut is known for many things: nutmeg, insurance, higher education, whaling, wealthy Gold Coasters. But one attribute that is not flattering would be Lyme disease. The potentially debilitating malady caused by the bite of the deer tick is named for the town where the first cases of this disease were recorded in 1975. A problem that some Connecticut residents wrestle with is the state's proximity to Plum Island. Is Lyme Disease just a bug carried by a bug or did it originate from testing done at Plum Island, a top-secret government research facility located just ten miles from the coast of Connecticut and only two from Long Island? Although technically a part of New York, the placement of this institution has had repercussions felt by Connecticut inhabitants.

The facility at Plum Island was opened in 1954 by the United States military. A former Nazi scientist, Dr. Eric Traub was one of the first doctors involved with Plum Island. Traub was recruited by the U.S. under its "Operation Paperclip," in which they granted clemency to German scientists who would work on the U.S.'s side in the burgeoning Cold War (even though some were involved with the horrors of Nazi scientific research).

Ironically, Plum Island is located close to the biggest American pro-Nazi camp and rallies, Camp Siegfried in Yaphank, New York. The Plum Island facility was built on the grounds of the former U.S. government Fort Terry, purchased during the Spanish-American War. The purpose of the research facility at Plum Island was to study animal diseases.

An Unidentified Animal

Plum Island had existed without much notice or public outcry until 2008, when a strange-looking creature nicknamed the "Montauk Monster" was found dead, washed ashore on a Montauk (Long Island) beach. The beast, which some say was a partially decayed or deformed commonplace animal such as a raccoon or a dog, looked unrecognizable.

Although its mid-sized body does resemble that of a common mammal, it has a beak-like skull. Due to the extent of its decomposition, it is plausible that the animal is ordinary, although skeptics feel that it is too much of a coincidence that an unidentifiable animal was washed ashore so close to the Plum Island research facility. They say that it was some kind of test victim that escaped the facility, or was mutated by something at the center, even though any wandering mammal (such as deer, which are actually known to be adept swimmers) to Plum Island would be killed onsite.

More Monsters

A second monster was found; this one was also bloated, but with fingers that looked like chicken feet. In early 2010, another oddity was found washed ashore. This one looked like a mutated human being with elongated fingers and holes drilled in its head, evidence for some that neurosurgery had been performed on it. Both creatures were bloated, and in stages of decomposition. What are these animals? Mammals? Turtles? A hybrid or a crossbreed? No one is certain. Since the first "monster sightings," other dead cryptozoological creatures have been seen in Connecticut (including at Silver Sands Beach in Milford) and Long Island, as well as elsewhere nationally and worldwide.

At the facility, there are 1,300 germ labs, although at the time of this writing, the whole island is up for sale with hopes that the Plum Island Center will be moved to Kansas. Critics say that Plum Island was not only the reason for the Lyme Disease epidemic, but also for the West Nile outbreak. At the facility, viruses are researched and created, so that scientists can then find defenses for them. Although security is tight, could one of those diseases have spread from Plum Island to the mainland?

Public visitation to Plum Island is forbidden, although it can be seen from the New London-Orient Point Ferry. Today the fate of Plum Island remains unknown. Will it move to Kansas and, for that matter, what becomes of an empty facility once strewn with legions of deadly viruses? Not even its prime location would entice buyers! In past years, Plum Island has been red-flagged for contamination complaints and dumped sewage. Even though the diseases being tested are supposedly ones that strictly infect animals, it is known that Lyme Disease has been studied there, and that emphatically affects humans.

In addition to the eerie knowledge that a government owned disease control center is located just a few miles off the shore of Connecticut and New York, there is a tale that an old sea captain haunts the island. A lone grave marks the spot of his final resting place.

While You're There:

The Book Barn

Check out The Book Barn in the Niantic section of East Lyme. This place is a literal maze of books. The Book Barn has three different locations, all in Niantic. The original store, located at 41 Main Street, comprises six different book houses, including the Haunted Building and Ellis Island (for new arrivals). Buildings are separated by genre, but be very specific: for example, there is a military history section, broken down into subdivisions. Closer to Niantic center, are the other two branches, named "Book Barn Downtown" and "Book Barn Midtown." It is best not to come with your heart set on one individual book; this place is suited for browsing—browsing that may take all afternoon. With couches, chairs, and snacks set up, The Book Barn encourages customers to take full advantage of the facility. Find well-chosen music and a plethora of pets located seemingly around every corner as the backdrop of your visit—you may not want to ever leave! The hallways and staircases tend to lead the customer every which way, so make sure to enjoy the meandering pace of the store. The knowledgeable and friendly staff will help with suggestions or let you know the availability of a title. The Haunted Book Shop may even be appropriately named, according to some customers.

7.
Stone Chambers, the Three-State Marker, and the Great Thompson Train Wreck

Location: Thompson

Near the abandoned Air Line Railroad in Thompson, Connecticut is a stone marker, about five feet tall, with the words, CONN, MASS, and RI, and the date 1883. The marker is located up a steep hill, following a rather difficult trail, with loose stones and tree roots.

A short way off the rail trail is a stone chamber, built into a small hill, fifteen feet across and seven to eight feet high at its peak. Two names are used to describe it: "Rocky Brook Chamber" and "Hermit's Cave."

One story claims that this was built by the Vikings, who were shipwrecked at Newport and made their way to Connecticut. Some say the stone chambers are merely root cellars, used for preserving food through the winter, but not all of the chambers were fully built into the ground, which weakens this theory. Some have compared the chambers to the stones of Stonehenge and similar sites in Ireland. On a guided walk of the area, the tour guide mentioned an Irish saying, "Two eleven-year-old boys with sharp sticks can hold off an army," suggesting that the stone chambers might have been used for defense.

The Air Line Trail is an extensive walking path trail that traverses much of the eastern part of the state. The main section in Thompson is the old railroad bed where the Great Thompson Train Wreck occurred. East Thompson was the location where two freight trains and two passenger trains smashed together on December 4, 1891. In a matter of five minutes, all four engines were destroyed, numerous people were injured, and miraculously, only two people were confirmed dead. The two freight trains first collided with one another, followed by the two passenger trains slamming into the wreck.

Whether walking on the path for history, exercise, or archaeoloy, this section of the Quiet Corner most certainly speaks volumes.

8.

The Other Side
of the Mohegan Tribe
Location: Montville

Today the Mohegan Tribe is known prominently for its world class casino, Mohegan Sun. Loads of gambling floors, premier entertainment venues, a professional women's basketball team, and top-tier restaurants all come to mind when mentioning the tribe and the casino. This section of the entry is the direct opposite of the gaming and the glitz of the 'Sun; it is a look at the traditional side of the Mohegan Tribe.

The best place to start for anyone curious about the tribe's history would be the Tantaquidgeon Museum. For visitors who have traveled up the road to the dazzling Mashantucket Pequot museum full of sights and sounds, a visit to the Tantaquidgeon Museum is the antithesis of that experience. For all the lavishness of the Mashantucket Pequot Museum, the Mohegans' historic museum brings none of this. It is housed in a simple stone and wood structure. The museum is the oldest Native American-run museum in the country, founded in 1931 by John Tantaquidgeon, who despite many physical limitations, including being on crutches and having sight in only one eye, built it with help from his son, Harold, and daughter, Gladys. Harold became chief of the tribe and Gladys became medicine woman, keeping records that would eventually go to help the cause of the Mohegan Tribe to achieve federal recognition. There is a life-size statue of Gladys in the Mohegan Sun Casino.

The museum houses artifacts and historical information relating to the Mohegan tribe.

The museum is open May to October from 10 to 4 and has free admission. The Tantaquidgeon Museum is located at 1814 Norwich-New London Turnpike in the Uncasville section of Montville.

Another visit to the other side of the Mohegan Reservation would be a trip to Cochegan Rock. Its location is one of its more interesting features. Cochegan Rock is the largest freestanding rock in the state. The boulder, or glacial rock, has existed in this location for about 17,000 years. The rock was measured in 1986 at 54 feet long, 50 feet high, 58 feet wide, weighing about 7,000 tons. All in all, it's quite a large rock! In 2008, the Mohegan Tribe bought this location that was sacred to them back from the Boy Scouts of America. Today, the land of the Rock is denoted by "No Trespassing" and "Reservation Land" signs.

Other than the obvious mass of the rock, another striking attribute of the site is how to get there. The path leading to the walk is only accessible from I-395 South in Montville. No, it is not off an exit; it is actually located behind the Mobil gas station and mini-mart. Park your car behind the Mobil and look for the clearing in the woods on the left of the green waste disposal containers. Walking from the lot to the rock, you will pass over a small bridge that spans a brook, quite a picturesque spot. Before reaching the rock, there are two decent-sized (think large, but not large compared to Cochegan Rock) rocks along the way. When the path forks, the trail leading to Cochegan Rock is on the right; soon after the split, the rock is on the left. Honestly, it is hard to miss. The large rock slopes at about a 45-degree angle. I was there on a rainy day and did not attempt a walk up the rock since I dared not chance my odds on a slick, fallen leaf-coated surface in the pouring rain. Also located nearby are old well-looking structures.

For more Mohegan attractions, visit Yantic Falls (included in another chapter) and the Royal Mohegan Burial Ground (including Uncas's grave), all in Norwich, as well as Fort Shantock State Park in Montville.

While You're There:

Mohegan Sun

Well, I guess this recommendation is inevitable, but, all in all, the Mohegan Sun does serve its purpose, to entertain. You are also able to have a good time at Mo-Sun on the cheap though, and not only by playing the penny slots all night. Putting a dollar or two on the horses at The Race Book is a fun alternative to the slot machines and table games. The Race Book also includes the casino's own brew pub featuring their own line of beers.

The Wolf Den has national headlining names play for free nightly; past unbelievable gratis shows have included acclaimed artists like George Clinton, Southside Johnny, and Deer Tick. Even expensive (but very tasty) restaurants like Michael Jordan's will run specials in off-times like a steak, side, and dessert combo for a reasonable sum.

The place to splurge, though, would be Leffingwell's Martini Bar. It is worth the $12 martini price tag to lounge in a plush, velvet chair and watch the overhead planetarium's sky change from day to night. The bar winds up three levels in a rock-like setting, reminding me of the Aggro Crag from Nickelodeon's *Guts* television show. (Maybe that is only after too many martinis....)

The casino is full of other establishments for food, drink, and entertainment, like the Dubliner Irish Bar, Trailblazer Outdoor Outfitters, and even a branch of New Haven's premier pizza joint, Frank Pepe Pizzeria (in addition to a *gazillion* slot machines and table games).

9.
Glacial Park
Location: Ledyard

Southeastern Connecticut is a veritable showcase of glacial rock debris. The sites along this tour include Gungywamp and Cochegan Rock. The granddaddy of them all would have to be Glacial Park in Ledyard. Located in a residential neighborhood off of Route 214, only a few miles away from the Groton border, this out-of-the-way park is a must-see for any geology fans. The parking lot is located off Whalehead Road. Park your car in the small dirt lot and look for the path. A boulder the size of a mobile home welcomes the visitor to the park. Follow the blue blazed trails to a veritable geological wonderland full of boulders and stones. Near the entrance to the park, the town has placed a bench to rest and observe the gigantic entrance stone. The initial boulders are slanted in the same directions, and with a close observation, glacial striations are visible.

Following the blue blazed trail left at the fork takes you to hillsides and a valley literally littered with Mini Cooper-sized rocks. Just before you reach this valley, you pass a cropping of rhododendron plants. (For other superb rhododendron locales, visit the Stamford Museum, the Rhododendron Sanctuary in Ledyard, and also the one at Gungywamp.) Once in the valley of the rocks, the previously well-blazed blue trail meanders to and fro, losing its clear path markings. The adventurous can hop from stone to stone, while other visitors may be advised to take their time walking around the rocks. A stone wall cuts through the valley, which makes an interesting contrast between the man-made wall and the natural rock-strewn land. Also, imagining this boulder-speckled land once being owned as someone's property is fascinating. Envision farming this rocky soil!

Standing in the midst of the rocky valley, you have 360 degrees of pure rock. The rocks come in all shapes and sizes, from large car-sized ones to small ones, easy to step upon. One of note resembled a boulder placed on a stone table. These rock creations were formed around 13,000 years ago by a melting glacier. The expanse of glacier rock is part of a boulder moraine, which is a spread of rock that is miles long and runs throughout the town of Ledyard. Thirteen thousand years ago, when the glacier stopped moving, this rocky moraine was formed at the edge of the glacier and left behind these large stone remains.

Other trails are located in the park, including the kettle hole trail, which is accessible from the Avery Road Extension. On the day of my visit, the atmosphere was incredibly serene. The only sound was a distant barking dog, and my companions and I were the only visitors. A visit to Glacial Park is recommended for anyone who is a geology fan or wants to take an interesting walk in the woods. On your way back from the park, notice the houses in the neighborhood that also have a glacial rock problem, some of which are dealt with very creatively. For a treat, take a drive down Sandy Hollow Road, passing by a picturesque lake on both sides that feels more like Maine than Connecticut.

The main entrance to the park is located on Whalehead Road in Ledyard, close to Routes 214, 12, and 127.

Ledyard's little known Glacial Park displaying the beauty of Mother Nature's masterpiece.

While You're There:

Mystic Disc

After you've spent your time looking at rocks, spend a while searching through the stacks of rock music at Mystic Disc. Located at 10 Steamboat Wharf in downtown Mystic, it's marked by a dummy sitting in a chair outside the door. The Disc specializes predominantly in vinyl. The styles vary, but the inventory tends to be heavy on the classic rock side, including imports and rare releases. Make sure to check out the local release section, as well as the world music, new releases, and discount section.

10.
Churaevka
Location: Southbury

What do the Constitution State and *War and Peace* have in common? You may first guess nothing, or maybe come up with a joke about both being "boring," but in reality, a small village in the town of Southbury was co-founded by Leo Tolstoy's son, Count Ilya Tolstoy. After fleeing Russia after the Bolshevik Revolution, Ilya Tolstoy came to the United States. He first lived in New York, but often found himself in Southbury while visiting his translator. When out strolling the woods near the Pomperaug River, he felt as if he were back in mother Russia and wanted to build a vacation residence, or a *dacha,* there. The area reminded him of the land where his family was from, over a hundred miles outside of Moscow. Wealthy Russian families often spent summers in a vacation home in that area.

Tolstoy founded the Russian Village of Churaevka in the town of Southbury with famous Siberian author George Grebenstchikoff, as an enclave for Russian creative types, such as artists, musicians, and scientists who were allowed to freely practice their craft.

The name "Churaevka" comes from the mythological Siberian village of Churaevei from one of Grebenstchikoff's books and is also inspired by the hometown of the author. Today, the most distinct feature of the Russian Village is the rubblestone chapel topped with a Russian Orthodox onion dome. The chapel was built between 1923 and 1933 and named for Saint Sergius of Radonega, who kept Christianity alive in Russia in the 1300s. The chapel was built by local volunteers and funded by the aircraft magnate, Igor Sikorsky. Nicholas Roerich, the Russian painter, writer, and philosopher, designed the chapel. Other famous Russians, including composer Sergei Rachmaninoff and actor Michael Chekhov, visited the village. In addition to residences and the chapel was the Alatas Print Shop, run by Grebenstchikoff, that would print his and other Russian authors' works. Churaevka, at one time, comprised over forty buildings and housed families all who were affected by strife in their home country. Today, the village is on the National Register of Historic Places.

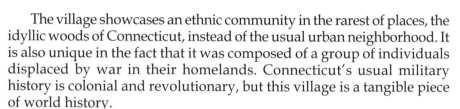

The village showcases an ethnic community in the rarest of places, the idyllic woods of Connecticut, instead of the usual urban neighborhood. It is also unique in the fact that it was composed of a group of individuals displaced by war in their homelands. Connecticut's usual military history is colonial and revolutionary, but this village is a tangible piece of world history.

Today, the village still contains summer cottages and year-round houses with a predominantly Russian Orthodox population. The chapel still stands and is used at different times throughout the year. The streets have names like Tolstoy Lane, Russian Village Road, and Kiev Drive. The village is located in a series of dead-end roads accessible by way of Ichabod Road and Main Street in Southbury. It literally stands in the shadow of Interstate 84 and is only a stone's throw away from Starbucks and The Gap, but at the same time, half a world away. If you get lost, just ask someone on the street for directions, unless they are "Russian," to get somewhere!

11.
Ballard Museum of Puppetry and Connecticut Archaeology Center

Location: Storrs

Majoring in puppetry is not a common career path at most American universities. This is not so at the University of Connecticut. In addition to having a degree program, UCONN also houses the Frank Ballard Museum of Puppetry. Ballard, a lifelong and world-renowned puppeteer, started the puppetry program at UCONN and was a professor there.

In addition to facts about Ballard and the history of the puppetry program, visitors to this museum get what they expect: lots of puppets. Most of these puppets are not the cute and fuzzy "Muppet" puppets (although they do have Scooter); but instead, you will find the kinds that might show up in a nightmare. Many of the puppets on display were used in UCONN productions. There are taped videos of past performances, old playbills, and other memorabilia. The puppets range in size from small shadow puppets to elaborate, enormous ones that are robed with much grandeur. Others are simple marionettes, with their dangling strings.

Through two good-sized rooms, the visitor will be shown the vast array of puppet types and sizes. The Ballard Institute holds programs for the public, as well. The museum is open seasonally on the weekends and by appointment. Next to Ballard is the former Mansfield Training School, a now-abandoned facility that housed cognitively delayed students. Today, its impressive architecture crumbles, along with many of the state's similar institutional buildings.

Soon, Ballard will be moving to the newly formed Storrs Center across the street from the UCONN campus on Route 195.
Note: The museum is NOT located on the main campus.

The Connecticut Archaeology Center

The Connecticut Archaeology Center is housed in the Connecticut State Museum of Natural History at the University of Connecticut at the main campus. The exhibit features the work of Dr. Nick Bellantoni, state archaeologist and professor at UCONN. The Center's exhibit, which is free to the public, contains artifacts and features several videos narrated by Dr. Bellantoni and other Connecticut experts who explore the connection between people and the environment. Dr. Bellantoni is a colorful person who engages visitors in this exhibit, as he presents topics including the way the climate controls our lives; how the use of land and water helped to shape the Industrial Revolution; and how nature's medicines, long utilized by Native Americans, are experiencing a revival today.

Dr. Bellantoni's live presentations are extremely dynamic, especially his talk on the Vampires of Jewett City (discussed in another chapter). He was also instrumental in the restoration of the gravesite of Samuel Huntington and his wife in the Norwichtown Burial Ground in Norwich. In a newsletter from the Museum of Natural History, Bellantoni asks:

What is this thing that makes those of us interested in archaeology compelled to play in the dirt? Well, it might be just that...play....Many folks who participate in Connecticut archaeology are "amateurs," which comes from the Latin "to love." When you "love"work, it can seem as "play."

In addition to field activities presented by the Museum of Natural History at UCONN, as well as other parts of the state, Bellantoni presents a series of lectures on such topics as Vampire Folk Beliefs in Historic New England and Victorian Gardens.

While You're There:

UCONN

The archaeology museum is located on UCONN's central campus. UCONN today is a well-regarded state school with superb academic programs and a premier athletic program, including the 2011 NCAA Men's Basketball champions. The central campus in Storrs is worth a stroll around while visiting either museum. UCONN's Co-op is a full-service bookstore and Husky memorabilia mecca. Many of the buildings, including the Co-op, are either recently built or renovated. There are two ponds on campus that are popular walking spots. Across the street is the UCONN Dairy Bar. UCONN started out as an agricultural school and this program is still a highly popular major for students. The ice cream at the dairy bar comes from the school's own cows. One warning: the sizes here are huge! A small size here compares to a large at other ice cream stands. A trip to UCONN would not be complete without a trip to the farm. Kids and adults will love to see the livestock including cows and sheep, whose voices ring out like a chorus from barns. Visitors are free to roam around the grounds themselves.

UCONN is located on Route 195 in Storrs.

12.
Camp Hadar
Location: Clinton

Classic summer camp locations tend to have an eerie feel about them (thanks to *Friday the 13th* and other such summer camp-based horror flicks), even when they are active. Is it the woods? Is it the shabby cabins? Is it the lack of parents? Most likely, it is all of those factors combined. If you have ever had the pleasure of walking through a protected wooded area during a non-summer month and have stumbled upon a smattering of cabins, mess halls, and other indicators of camp use, you may have been a little reluctant to press ahead. The vacant camp site is chilling; it is almost like being a visitor in a post-apocalyptic city—the facilities still in working condition, but no humans in sight.

The former Camp Hadar in Clinton is an extreme version of this. The icing on the cake is that Camp Hadar has been closed since the '90s, but the buildings are still standing. Furthermore, it looks as if the camp has only adjourned for the season—not forever. The camp sits on ninety-seven acres and was a Jewish summer camp from the World War I years, until it closed in the mid-1990s. Before the Great Depression, it was also home to the Carter Farm, which was a major American corn producer. Today, the property still encompasses a camp full of unoccupied summer camp buildings. There have been unsuccessful bids on redevelopment into other uses for the space in the past, but so far nothing permanent.

13.
Civilian Conservation Corps Museum
Location: Stafford Springs

A look into the daily life of a member of the Civilian Conservation Corps. This display is located at the CCC Museum in Stafford Springs.

In the 1930s, at the height of the Great Depression, Franklin Delano Roosevelt created programs to get America working and to, in turn, stimulate the economy. Organizations like the WPA, TVA, and CCC were created. The CCC, Civilian Conservation Corps, was prominent in Connecticut and was a place that housed many of the states' young men. At these camps, the men who lived and worked there had regimented lives, with communal meals, structured routines, and cooperative projects. At the CCC, men learned trades, trades that could be taken and turned into jobs after they left.

The CCC had campsites all over the state of Connecticut, adjoined to state parks. Camp Conner was located in Shenipsit State Forest, in Stafford Springs (and is the current location of the CCC Museum); Camp Lonergan was in Voluntown in Pachaug State Forest; and Camp Stuart was situated in the Salmon River State Forest in East Hampton.

Camp Lonergan was the longest running CCC camp; it ran for nine years from 1933 to 1942. Only thirty-four days after FDR was sworn in as President, he created the CCC camps. The men at Lonergan built bridges, dams, and trails through the woods of Pachaug. These camps were places where boys could learn skills to become successful adults in the working world. The men had specialized jobs like carpenter, truck

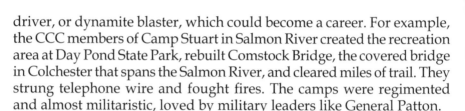

driver, or dynamite blaster, which could become a career. For example, the CCC members of Camp Stuart in Salmon River created the recreation area at Day Pond State Park, rebuilt Comstock Bridge, the covered bridge in Colchester that spans the Salmon River, and cleared miles of trail. They strung telephone wire and fought fires. The camps were regimented and almost militaristic, loved by military leaders like General Patton.

The camps were located across the nation and employed 3.5 million men. There were regulations about joining a camp. Boys had to be at least 17 years old to sign up. They needed to weigh at least 107 pounds, be at least five-feet tall, and have at least three working teeth. The harsh realities of the Great Depression were that many of the recruits were too thin from not having enough food to eat and had to go to a conditioning camp before joining the CCC. Since the work they did was manual labor, not easy work, they needed to be able to perform the needed tasks. For some of the men at the camp, this was the first time they had ever seen a real doctor or dentist! The most important stipulation to joining was that the family needed to be "on dole" to be eligible for the camp. Dole was the term for welfare or government assistance back then. The men earned a dollar a day for their work and had to send $25 home to help their family. The camps were year-round and each camp in Connecticut housed 200 teenage boys. They were racially integrated before the military was, where men of any color were allowed to bunk, work, and live together. While at camp, the men had plenty of food to eat, as daily meals were always provided. The men joined baseball and football teams while at camp. In Connecticut, there were twenty-one camps altogether.

At a time when unemployment was at twenty-five percent in the United States, "Roosevelt's Tree Army" numbered 3.5 million men nationwide. They planted three billion trees, built parks, dams, roads, bridges, and buildings over a nine-year period from 1933 to 1942. One famous ex-Corps member was actor Walter Mathau.

The CCC Museum is an interesting look inside the life of a civilian of the CCC, an often overlooked program of FDR to stimulate the economy and curtail unemployment.

Inside the museum, the visitor can view all kinds of CCC memorabilia from group photographs and camp pamphlets to sports jerseys and meal menus. The guide was extremely informative, showing me all around the museum and sharing many stories. For a look into the lives of many of our fathers and grandfathers, my grandfather included, a trip to this museum is a must.

The museum is located in the town of Stafford Springs, right off Route 190 in Shenipsit State Forest at the former headquarters of Camp Conner. It is only open on the weekends.

14.
The Danbury Railway Museum
Location: Danbury

The railroad is an integral part of the history of the United States; its rise made the nation grow at an outstanding rate. As train use became more popular, travel time shrank drastically, which benefitted all walks of society. The railroad helped give a boost to a new tourism industry in the 1800s, and it caused business to grow rapidly with a faster method to receive and ship products. The railroad industry employed thousands, from steel workers, to conductors, to CEOs, to newly arrived immigrants. A more localized version of the train, the streetcar, caused cities to sprawl miles beyond their original borders, helping to provide new and far-reaching housing for workers commuting from outside of center city.

In terms of western Connecticut, it brought areas like Greenwich, Fairfield, and Danbury much closer to the king of American cities, its neighbor to the west, New York City. One example is the factory town of Danbury, which became a crucial stop along the New York, New Haven, and Hartford Railroad. Danbury, which had already established itself as a major hat-producing city, benefitted even more from the expedited service of the railroad. Other towns that happened to be situated on a railroad line flourished solely due to their newfound beneficial location.

As the years went on, train travel was replaced by airplanes for long-distance trips, and Americans found themselves relying more on their cars than on public transit for covering smaller distances. The railroad industry went into a period of decline, with lines like the Norwich-Worcester and the aforementioned New York, New Haven, and Hartford Railroad being discontinued for passenger service. Beautiful stations, some even designed by world-renown architects like Henry Hobson Richardson, were left vacant and, in some circumstances, fell into disrepair.

Danbury's Union Station is a prime example of one such train station. The Metro North railway is a commuter line that runs from outlying areas of New York into midtown. Connecticut's New Haven Line is appropriately named since its terminus is New Haven, but it does have a branch off the shoreline route, which veers north from South Norwalk up to Danbury, passing through towns like New Canaan, Wilton, and Bethel. Metro North discontinued Danbury's Union Station for active use in 1993. This Richardsonian Romanesque-styled train station was built in 1903 and has a classic look to it. It was even used as the station in Alfred Hitchcock's classic film *Strangers on a Train*. Because it had been such an essential feature of the city for so long, and due to its status as

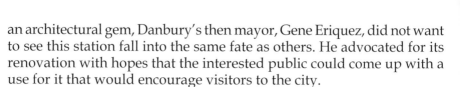

an architectural gem, Danbury's then mayor, Gene Eriquez, did not want to see this station fall into the same fate as others. He advocated for its renovation with hopes that the interested public could come up with a use for it that would encourage visitors to the city.

The Danbury Railroad Museum was incorporated in 1994, but was located in a small space in downtown Danbury until 1996. After the closing of Union Station for active use, it was rehabilitated for use as the showcase of the railroad museum. Today, the station is only one part of the multi-faceted attraction. There are about sixty pieces of train and train equipment on display. The most crowd-gathering aspect of the museum is the train ride that can be taken by the public on a twenty-minute jaunt around the rail yard. The rides are staged from April to November. Kids and adults alike will be delighted with a look at an authentic steam engine. There are many discontinued train cars to be viewed, including a caboose. Seasonal favorites include a train ride with the Easter Bunny and a pumpkin patch ride where kids get a free pumpkin, as well as apple cider for all! Where passengers used to wait for the train inside of Union Station is now the main display area for the museum. In addition to the train cars and engines, also on display are electric trains, some of which are available for purchase, among many other gifts in the museum store. (Included at the store were even Thomas the Tank themed toys and gadgets.)

The Danbury Railway Museum is located at 120 White Street, close to Interstate 84 in Danbury.

A steam-driven locomotive thunders its way from Essex up the Connecticut River, carrying train enthusiasts and children of all ages for a scenic journey into the past. The Essex Steam Train and Riverboat is located in Essex.

Other Train Museums

Essex Steam Train
The Connecticut Trolley Museum
Connecticut Eastern Railroad Museum
The Railroad Museum of New England
Shoreline Trolley Museum

If you are not *all train-ed out* after a trip to the Railway Museum, combine this with any of Connecticut's other train locations, like the Essex Steam Train, The Connecticut Trolley Museum in East Windsor, Connecticut Eastern Railroad Museum in Willimantic, the Railroad Museum of New England in Thomaston, or the Shoreline Trolley Museum in Branford. Trains are fascinating to all ages; the appeal of the iron horses bridge any generation gap.

15.
The Military Museum of Southern New England
Location: Danbury

Have you ever wanted to jump into the driver's seat of a tank? Visit The Military Museum of Southern New England on one of its Open Turret days to do just that! Once a month, the museum puts its visitors in the drivers' seats of certain vehicles in their impressive convoy.

The museum was founded in 1995, in remembrance of the legacy created by this country's heroes, to reflect on its past, and to provide a place that history can be literally grasped. The front outside area of the museum, surrounded by a chain-link fence, is a parking lot for numerous martial modes of transport, including a slew of tanks, tank destroyers, and armored vehicles ranging from World War I to today. The museum even has a Soviet armored car that was captured by U.S. forces during the Korean War. The assortment not only includes Allied weaponry, but enemies' equipment as well. The vehicle collection is among the finest and largest in the country.

Inside the museum are dioramas staged by mannequins in various combat poses, depicting different scenes from prior wars. The panoramas extend onto the surrounding walls with painted images as a continuation of the same scene. The museum is staffed by volunteers, about seventy-five of them in all, whose duties range from maintaining the fleet and lending their artistic talents to the indoor displays, to staffing the gift shop and selling tickets. An artist has also created miniature dioramas with exquisite detail, which are about the size of a toy model display. It is a unique place that shows the visitor truly what role equipment, soldiers, and vehicles had throughout the history of modern American warfare. Also on site is a library with tons of books on military history and a function room where war board games are played on a weekly basis. The museum even holds birthday parties!

A movable museum, which is actually a refurbished army truck whose bed now holds a portable collection, allows staff to give educational talks at local schools and for community groups.

The Military Museum of Southern New England is located in Danbury at 125 Park Avenue. Adults pay $6 to enter. From April through November, the museum is open Tuesday through Sunday, and in December to March, it is open only Friday through Sunday. Look at their website (www.usmilitarymuseum.org) for dates and times of the monthly Open Turret days that enable visitors to venture into a vehicle for themselves.

16.
Two Offbeat Museums: Vintage Radios and Tobacco
Location: Windsor

Windsor is home to two museums with a very specific focus: The Vintage Radios and Communication Museum of Connecticut and The Luddy/Taylor Connecticut Valley Tobacco Museum.

The Vintage Radios and Communication Museum of Connecticut

The Vintage Radio Museum's collection includes antique communication devices such as televisions, computers, radios, and memorabilia like large Zenith television signs. Visitors can listen to a radio broadcast from 1926 and to hand-cranked Victrolas spinning the top tunes of 1910. Exhibits feature one particular mechanism, for instance: a glass display case with various tubes that are used in televisions, guitar amps, and radios.

The word "vintage" has different meanings for various age groups. For most of the visiting populace, gramophones would certainly classify as vintage, but for the younger set, turntables and 1980s computers are considered "vintage." The museum even showcases the importance of communication devices in terms of the military. They have the Eppley Standard Cell Laboratory, which, at the time of this writing, was kept in storage, awaiting restoration.

The museum somewhat resembles the audio/visual section of the local Goodwill—a hodgepodge of dusty equipment (sans the dust) and the DVD players are replaced with gramophones and ham radios. If you happen to have your ham radio license, there is a ham radio station or "shack" called W1VCM onsite.

Move over Cooperstown or Springfield or Cleveland! This museum houses a more obscure Hall of Fame: the Connecticut Broadcasters Hall of Fame! Vote for your favorite CT Broadcaster! The recording studio is a really neat section of the museum. This recording studio has equipment circa 1970 that can still be rented out today to record bands and the like. The equipment is all vintage, with the newest pieces being from the 1980s, but much of it from the '70s, '60s, and even earlier decades. The music can even be recorded on reel to reel! It is time to get the band back together for a recording session at the museum's studio!

The Vintage Radio and Communication Museum of Connecticut first opened its doors in 1990 in New Britain. The museum changed locales over the years, including a stay in East Hartford and other locations in Windsor.

Today's museum, located on 115 Pierson Lane, in Windsor, first opened its doors in 2007. The museum is open from Thursday to Sunday, and regular admission is $7 at the time of this writing. On your way out, make sure to check out the gift shop, including museum memorabilia. Who wouldn't want a Philco 90 vintage radio t-shirt or hat?

Luddy/Taylor Connecticut Valley Tobacco Museum

If you are a cigar-smoking, vintage radio-phile, Windsor is the place for you! After the first stop at the CVRCM (Connecticut Vintage Radio and Communication Museum), the next destination is the Luddy/Taylor Connecticut Valley Tobacco Museum. Did you know that, in 1763, Israel Putnam was the first person in New England to come up with the idea of smoking rolled leaves as a cigar? At this museum, the visitor will learn the history of the special shade tobacco that grows natively in the Connecticut River Valley from Portland, Connecticut, up to Lower Vermont, which is used to wrap some of the world's finest cigars.

The museum's collection is housed in two tobacco sheds, one restored genuine shed and one replica. The tobacco from the Connecticut Valley was always considered top quality. In the late 1800s, a new kind of tobacco leaf from Sumatra (an island in Indonesia) was the champion of the cigar industry. A technique that was employed in the Connecticut Valley was protecting the plants from the hot summer sun by placing the plants under the guard of a white tent. The man responsible for selling these tents was John E. Luddy, who, after his passing, left money to fund the museum. Inside the museum is equipment related to the tobacco industry, with live tobacco plants, photos, and writing about Connecticut Valley tobacco. The area's industry is about 2,000 acres, shrunk from what, at its peak, was 30,000 acres.

The Luddy/Taylor Connecticut Valley Tobacco Museum is open on Tuesdays, Wednesdays, Thursdays, and Saturday from 12-4, March through December. The museum is located in Northwest Park at 135 Lang Road in Windsor.

While You're There:

New England Air Museum
Located close by, in the town of Windsor Locks, is the New England Air Museum. Featuring a topic that may appeal to more mainstream audiences than tobacco or vintage radios, the Air Museum consists of numerous flight-related objects, including a collection of 125 planes (not all of which are on display). From early Wright Brothers-styled planes to military jets, the museum features a vast array of airplanes and other aviation-themed exhibits.

The museum is located at Bradley International Airport.

17.
Factories, Frogs, and Foliage
Location: Willimantic/Windham

Mills were the heartbeat of much of Connecticut's economy. They were situated on rivers like the Shetucket, Housatonic, Naugatuck, and Quinnebaug, which became the economic lifeblood of the state. One of the most impressive mills was the Ponemah Mill in Taftville, Connecticut. It was the largest single cotton-producing building in the nation. Mills brought in a new wave of immigration to Connecticut. Different towns attracted different ethnicities, such as French Canadians in the northeast and Polish in New Britain. Today, more often than not, the mills still exist, either as shells of their former selves, or as rehabbed and redeveloped modern facilities.

The rivers that make up the Quinnebaug-Shetucket National Corridor have mill towns that dot the banks every few miles. Some have recovered from the companies fleeing the area and have reinvented themselves, best exemplified by Putnam becoming the antique mecca of New England. Others have fallen into deep financial ruin, such as North Grosvenordale and Jewett City, while others have straddled the line somewhere in between like Norwich and Willimantic.

Willimantic, known mostly for frogs and thread, was a once-booming mill town that currently is slowly revitalizing itself with culture and cuisine. Traditions such as the Willimantic Boom Box Parade, sponsored by local radio station WILI once a year, encourage residents and visitors to take to the streets wearing red, white, and blue, and march in a parade every Fourth of July, equipped with boom boxes, all tuned to AM 1400. Other festivities include Willimantic's Third Thursdays art and music celebrations. It is home to a microbrewery, Willimantic Brewing Company, and Eastern Connecticut State University, as well as a few boutiques and restaurants. The American Thread Company, a beautiful nineteenth century stone mill, which was once the city's main employer, sits on the edge of downtown, majestically overlooking the town, recently restored as an Artspace community.

Across the street from this grandiose mill is the Windham Textile Museum. Located on Route 66 in the Willimantic section of Windham, this museum is housed in a former smaller mill building. As visitors enter the ground level, they enter a gift shop full of Willimantic-themed items, including "Romantic Willimantic" t-shirts, books, and jewelry. The museum is located on the two upper floors of this building and in the nineteenth century factory building next door.

On the second floor of the museum is an interesting exhibit called "Textile Town." Textiles were the main product manufactured along the rivers in New England. Another name for cloth, some mills spun yarn and thread, some dyed fabric, and some bleached cloth. Textile Town shows the visitor what life was like for the worker and manager of a typical New England textile mill. The scene being depicted happens to be that of workers of the American Thread Company. As the visitor climbs the staircase, he or she enters a "street" with facades of buildings facing the hallway. Visits into these rooms showcase different aspects of mill workers' factory and home lives. One room displays all kinds of sewing machines that could have been used in a textile factory. Another room shows what a house of a worker was like, with cramped quarters for many people. Another depicts the more lavish lifestyle of an owner or factory manager. Along the walls are pictures of Victorian-era Willimantic, the town in a more prosperous time. The staircase of the third floor of the museum is lined with photos of various places of worship in Willimantic. From Irish and Eastern European churches near the bottom to Hispanic and African American near the top, the pictures represent the various waves of immigration into the Thread City.

The third floor, called Dunham Hall, acts as a library full of books about the town, as well as mill life. The attic also contains textile machinery. Located next door is the Dugan Mill, where the visitor can observe authentic tools from the Industrial Revolution used at American Thread during its time as a working and thriving factory.

The mills and factories of New England are historical testaments similar to castles or feudal manors. They are truly history incarnate. What makes the Windham Textile Museum so special is that the visitor is allowed to time travel and step inside the home and workplace of a nineteenth-century textile worker. It lets the visitor physically grasp an important piece of the history of this country.

During my visit to the second floor of the museum, I felt eerily alone, even though I was with three people. Venturing into rooms by myself, the presence of creepy mannequins and mirrors was unnerving, almost as if someone were viewing my every move. Only much later did I find out the museum is allegedly haunted, with strange occurrences like odd noises, objects being tampered with, cold spots, and reports of feeling watched. After gaining this information, I felt relieved that it was not only me that sensed something strange in the Windham Textile and History Museum.

The solo visitor doesn't feel alone in the Windham Textile Museum due to the mannequins and other worldly presence. Windham Textile Museum is located in the Willimantic section of Windham.

The Windham Textile Museum is located on Route 66 in the Willimantic section of Windham. If you are traveling from the south, you will arrive in the center of Willimantic via Route 32.

Crossing into Willimantic, you will see a curious sight literally sitting atop the bridge spanning the Willimantic River. There is a set of four frog statues, each resting on a large spool of thread on each side of both ends of the bridge. So far the spools of thread make sense, but why the frogs you ask?

During the end of the French and Indian War, tensions were high in the villages of Connecticut, for the fear of a Native American attack was ever present. One evening, the town of Windham was witness to horrible ominous sounds reverberating through town. Some villagers thought it was the rapture; others were sure it was a siege on the village. The next morning, the culprits were found. The legend says that hundreds or maybe even thousands of bullfrog carcasses lay strewn on the edge of Dyer's Pond. The enemy attack was actually fighting amphibians. The pond had been drying up due to severe drought, and the frog community was battling it out to claim the remaining water. The casualties of the fight lined the edge of the pond. So the horrible sounds from the night before were in some way an attack, and the end of days, but only for the town's frog population. This story of the Windham Frog Fight explains the frog on the town emblem and the giant statues that line "frog bridge."

Across from the Frog Bridge lies Jillson Square. All that is left of this once-thriving community is an abandoned movie theater. Like many American cities, Willimantic went through a period of urban renewal. In the late 1960s and early 1970s, the old center was demolished, but nothing was ever done with the land, except for the now-closed, dilapidated cinema.

The Air Line Trail, an old train line that has been converted into a multi-use trail for bikers, walkers, and runners, begins in East Hampton and travels its way through the eastern half of the state, chugging its way through the towns of Hebron, Lebanon, and Colchester before terminating in Thompson. The trail continues through Massachusetts to the town of Franklin, where it is known as the Southern New England Trunkline Trail.

Willimantic's most famous landmark, The Frog Bridge, commemorates two important events in its history: the Windham frog fight and the spool its sits upon representing Windham's textile and thread-making past.

Currently, the Air Line Trail is chunked into two parts. The southern part runs from East Hampton to Lebanon, and the northern branch goes from Willimantic to Putnam, as well as an extension from Thompson to the Massachusetts border. Hopefully, the trail locations will some day be linked to make a continuous path. The trail crosses rivers, bridges, towns, and forest. Taking the northern section of the trail from its Willimantic beginning, about a half mile in, just after exiting Willimantic proper, you will find an amazing view of the Natchaug River. The Natchaug, which is often hidden from street views, is nestled into the woods. This picturesque spot on the former railway bed is especially beautiful in the fall, where the overhanging trees on the Natchaug turn an explosion of autumn color.

A view of Willimantic's "Lost River" (Natchaug River) along the Windham branch of the Air Line State Park Trail.

Speaking of trains, another off the beaten path Willimantic attraction is the Connecticut Eastern Railroad Museum. This museum, only open weekends from Labor Day through the end of October, houses many pieces of train equipment including train cars and even the former Chaplin (CT) station!

While You're There:

Willimantic Brewing Company/ Main Street Café

If touring all of the history in this town makes you thirsty and/or hungry, stop in at the Willimantic Brewing Company/Main Street Café. With locally themed meal choices, including the Fitchville Fried Calamari and the Mansfield Flank Steak, this former post office includes even the village zip codes next to the menu choice. The Willimantic Brewing Company brews its own delicious beer. The mainstays include an IPA, Stout, and their flagship beer, "Certified Gold." Look for their seasonal selection too, which may include a barleywine or a saison.

18.
Carousel, Clock, and Watch Museums
Location: Bristol and Waterbury

Timexpo, The Timex Museum

Timexpo, The Timex Museum, is located in an old factory in Waterbury. The three-floor exhibit traces the Timex heritage, from its roots in the 1850s to the very latest innovations. From displays of World War I wrist watches and early pocket watches to projections of future watches, the museum has something for everyone. There are interactive displays for children, including an area where they are given white cardboard wrist bands that they can stamp and customize to create their own watches. The exhibit of Mickey Mouse watches will fascinate the kids as well as parents, with a detailed description of the company's near financial ruin of 1929, when the brilliant decision was made to buy the rights to the Mickey Mouse watch—and the rest is history.

An Easter Island Statue in front of Waterbury's Time Expo Museum.

In addition to beautiful clock displays, the Time Tunnel area allows the participant to travel back to the ancient world to marvel at the mysteries of Easter Island and connections across the seas. There is a replica of an Easter Island figure inside the museum, as well as a huge version on the lawn. An exhibit of the North American Mounds features a wall painting depicting a flourishing early civilization. For the baby boomer generation, you can view television commercials featuring John Cameron Swayze demonstrating how the Timex watch "takes a licking and keeps on ticking." The humorous commercials feature Timex watches being shaken by an outboard motor, driven over by a car, and lost in a sixteen wheeler's tire for hundreds of miles. This is a nicely designed, fun museum.

The Timexpo Museum is located at 175 Union Street in Waterbury.

The New England Carousel Museum

The New England Carousel Museum in Bristol is a delight for children of all ages. There are hundreds of carousel horses and other carousel figures, dating from the 1800s to the present time. The craft of the horse carvers is explained in a fascinating tour of the museum, and the various styles of the carvers and decorators are illustrated. From the simple country fair-style horses, designed to be stacked quickly in order to move from fair to fair, to the highly ornate Coney Island style, featuring an abundance of jewels and gold leaf, the tour guide's explanations help the viewer focus on unique aspects of the various styles of horses. The Carousel Museum manages and runs the Historic Bushnell Park Carousel in Hartford, with its 48 horses, 2 chariots, and a wonderful Wurlitzer Band Organ. The carousel, 100 years old in 2014, is one of the premier attractions in downtown Hartford.

The New England Carousel Museum is located at 95 Riverside Avenue in Bristol. The second floor of the museum houses two small museums, The Museum of Fire History and the Greek Museum of Art and History, and includes a huge open space with newly refurbished wood floors. This area can be rented for private functions.

A look inside Bristol's Carousel Museum.

American Clock and Watch Museum

Also in Bristol is the American Clock and Watch Museum. The museum is literally strewn with clocks of all shapes and sizes, from grandfather clocks to wrist watches. It features American-made time pieces and has a special focus on Connecticut-based manufacturers.

You will not have to ask anyone for the time here since there are about 1,500 clocks and watches on display. The museum houses a permanent collection, as well as rotating exhibits. During my visit, the featured galleries included "Women in the Clock Industry" and "Connecticut Clockmaking and the Industrial Revolution." The gift shop had an extensive selection of clock and watch related gift items with a broad book section.

The American Clock and Watch Museum is at 100 Maple Street in Bristol.

While You're There:

Ted's Restaurant

Stop for lunch at Ted's Restaurant in Meriden, home of the steamed cheeseburger. A small area of central Connecticut is known for this unusual burger. The burger is cooked through (no medium rare here), and the steamed cheese placed on the meat resembles molten lava. This restaurant, with its small counter, and four booths, also features home fries that may be drenched with the hot cheese. The prices on the small menu make you feel that a time machine has dropped you into the 1950s!

Ted's is located at 1046 Broad Street in Meriden.

19.
Doll Museums

Location: Coventry, Preston

Have you ever looked into the lifeless face of a doll and averted your eyes because you have felt more than slightly uncomfortable? Whether it is because of popular culture with "Chucky" from the *Child's Play* movie series or a fear of clowns, these popular subjects of children's nightmares are often presented as quite scary.

Although not meant to be frightening, Special Joys Doll and Toy Museum in Coventry has a wide range of dolls on display and for sale. Housed in a large, pink Victorian house, half of it is used as a bed and breakfast, while the other part is the store and museum. Typically, doll museums showcase classic porcelain figurines, which Special Joys does,

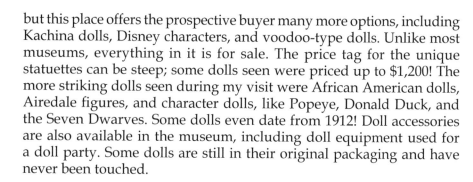

but this place offers the prospective buyer many more options, including Kachina dolls, Disney characters, and voodoo-type dolls. Unlike most museums, everything in it is for sale. The price tag for the unique statuettes can be steep; some dolls seen were priced up to $1,200! The more striking dolls seen during my visit were African American dolls, Airedale figures, and character dolls, like Popeye, Donald Duck, and the Seven Dwarves. Some dolls even date from 1912! Doll accessories are also available in the museum, including doll equipment used for a doll party. Some dolls are still in their original packaging and have never been touched.

Special Joys is located at 41 North River Road in Coventry.

Preston's Young at Heart Doll Shop

Can't get enough doll shops? Look no further: Connecticut is also home to Preston's Young at Heart Doll Shop on Route 2. It is located in a dilapidated strip mall called the Tally-Ho Mall and marked by a sign that says "2000 Dolls." From Cabbage Patch to porcelain, from Native American to character dolls, this doll shop really has what the doll lover is looking for.

The store, on Route 2, is open Fridays and Saturdays, from May to December.

20.
A Town of New Heights
Location: Simsbury

Nestled inside Talcott Mountain State Park, just off Route 185 on the Simsbury side of its border with Bloomfiend, is the Heublein Tower. The tower rises 980 feet above sea level and 165 feet above the ground. It has been likened to Bavarian and Tyrolean castles of central Europe. Visitors can climb up the 120 steps to the glass observation room, which, on a clear day, grants views as far off as Long Island and the Berkshire Hills.

Built in 1914, the tower served as a summer retreat for the Heublein family, of the Heublein Liquor and Food Distribution fame (which marketed taste treats like A-1 Steak Sauce, Smirnoff vodka, and pre-mixed versions of Sidecars, Martinis, and Manhattans). The first stories of the building are made of stone, while the massive tower protruding from the lower levels looks like a stouter version of Provincetown's Pilgrim Monument or Waterbury's Union Station. Heublein's color is completely white and has a larger top than the others, as well as a red cross gabled roof and cupola along with the glass observatory. Towers have been erected at this same locale since the first was built in 1810, with even Mark Twain as a visitor.

The state has owned the park and tower since 1966, and the tower is run by the "Friends of Heublein Tower." A visit to the tower not only rewards spectacular views, but a trip inside it shows rooms equipped with period furnishings. The most popular time to visit is in the fall; it gets especially busy on the weekends during the leaf-peeping season. The tower is open from Memorial Day through the last weekend in October. A trail that is accessible to the tower is the aptly named "Tower Trail," which leads hikers in the state park to it. The Heublein Tower affords visitors an economical way to see stunning views and Bavarian-style architecture for less than a penny.

> **Warning:** The Tower Trail from the parking lot to the tower is incredibly steep, long (1.25 miles), and rocky!

The Pinchot Sycamore

The Heublein Tower is not the only tall object in Simsbury. The Pinchot Sycamore tree measures some 26 feet around, 93 feet high, and has a canopy of 138 feet (at the last time of official measurement), was named for Gifford Pinchot (not for Bronson, sorry *Perfect Strangers* fans), a local conservationist turned co-founder of Yale's forestry program and eventual Pennsylvania governor. So, if you are looking for a natural "high," Simsbury is a good place to start!

> Located in a small park along the Farmington River in the Weatogue section of the town, the Pinchot Sycamore is the largest tree in Connecticut.

21.
Gillette Castle
Location: East Haddam

Not so deep into the Connecticut woods, on the banks of the Connecticut River, perched high atop the chain of hills known as the Seven Sisters, is Gillette Castle. This castle, and yes it is a castle, was built in 1913 at the request of William Gillette. Gillette was famous for portraying Sherlock Holmes on stage. His vision of his dream house came to him while docking his houseboat on the Connecticut River, at the bottom of the Seven Sisters. He decided to build his home on the tallest hill and name his creation The Seventh Sister. Gillette scrapped his earlier plan of building on Long Island as soon as he realized the majesty that could rise from the hills of his home state. He spent over a million dollars on the home and its 122 adjoining acres.

Gillette was born in Hartford, Connecticut, to a rich politician on July 24, 1853, and was a descendant of the famous Hooker family (of the Governor Hooker fame). William was the youngest of six children. His father wanted him to be a man of politics like himself. William had other plans, and aspired to be an actor and writer, due to the urging of the Gillettes' neighbor, Mark Twain. His New York City debut came in 1877 in an adaptation of Mark Twain's *The Gilded Age*, followed by a play that Gillette penned himself called *The Professor*.

The actor William Gillette, known for his portrayal of Sherlock Holmes, built his dream "castle" in the hills of East Haddam overlooking the Connecticut River.

Much of his early work brought Gillette fame and fortune, but was not critically acclaimed. On a tour of one of his lesser known plays, a young actor named Charles Chaplin was chosen as a cast member. Much to his chagrin, Gillette was forced to take a six-year hiatus from theater due in part to an illness, but he returned to the stage in the late 1890s.

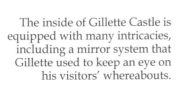

His manager got the rights to Sir Arthur Conan Doyle's *Sherlock Holmes*, and Gillette worked on revising the script, but after completing it in 1897, bad luck struck, and the script burned in a hotel fire. After another rewriting, the play opened in Buffalo, New York, in 1897. Gillette's run as Sherlock Holmes made him the most recognizable actor to play the part. It was Gillette himself who gave Holmes the now clichéd "deerstalker" hat and pipe, and this image became the model for many illustrators of Sherlock Holmes books. Gillette's run as Holmes lasted decades, even as he forayed slightly into silent motion picture acting, and became the first voice of Holmes on CBS radio. Gillette played the role over 1,300 times, in numerous cities, including New York and London. Gillette was only married for six years, when his wife, Helen Nickels, originally from Detroit, Michigan, tragically passed away. Although he never remarried, rumor was he did not lack for female companionship.

Gillette's faux-German castle is built from Connecticut fieldstone and white oak from Georgia. The rocks had to be brought up the large hill by a tram system. The castle is chock-full of all kinds of gizmos, including secret panels and a mirror system, which the eccentric Gillette used to spy on his guests. From his bedroom, Gillette could see via mirrors who was helping himself to a drink at his bar. He could also see who was arriving in the great hall, so that he could stage a grandiose entrance. There are forty-seven hand-carved doors in the castle, all with intricate locks. The locks and light switches, all made of wood, are extremely ornate. The minute details of the castle's interior are dumb-founding. For example, in the downstairs study, his desk chair is on a guided track so as not to scratch the floor. He installed an intricate sprinkler system throughout the castle, in which pipes were set up with wooden tassels to pull in case of a fire. Upstairs, there is a tower room with windows facing three sides, providing an incredible view of the Connecticut River.

The inside of Gillette Castle is equipped with many intricacies, including a mirror system that Gillette used to keep an eye on his visitors' whereabouts.

One of the rooms is set up just like Sherlock Holmes's study, and occasionally an actor is hired to portray William Gillette portraying Sherlock Holmes. The castle also features wooden light switches, and a room that he would scurry into if someone appeared at his front door whom he wanted to avoid.

Gillette was obsessed with cats as well as frogs. His adoration can be seen in the copious amount of feline and frog memorabilia strewn around the castle. From pictures to figurines, the visitor will encounter them at every turn. Before the recent renovation to the castle, there used to be a frog fountain at the side of the castle, with water spurting from the frog's mouth. One of the most interesting rooms in the castle is the greenhouse-styled room, equipped with a lovely waterfall and a frog pond for Gillette's two pet frogs. Gillette also fancied trains, hence the three-mile narrow gauge rail loop on the grounds. The train traveled under tunnels and over bridges. There are tales of Gillette driving friends in one of two locomotives on crazy rides throughout his many acres. One of his trains was later sold to Lake Compounce Park in Bristol, Connecticut. Mr. Gillette also had a riverboat docked at the foot of his property on the Connecticut River. On the grounds is Grand Central Station (for the train), which is now a picnic area, and a frog pond. In his time living in the Seventh Sister, he entertained well-known figures, like the aforementioned Charlie Chaplin and Albert Einstein.

Gillette Castle is a fascinating combination of a man seemingly more child than adult. William retained his youthful vigor and enthusiasm late into his years, especially given the fact that his dream home was not even built until he was well into his sixties. In Gillette's case, he had a plentiful amount of money and used it to its fullest. Every childhood hobby and dream became a reality. He liked trains, as do many children, but as most do not get to do, he bought two real working locomotives and designed a three-mile narrow gauge around his "yard" so that he could become a train conductor. While considered by some to be merely a Connecticut eccentric, Gillette must be given credit for being true to himself. Expensive clothing, jewels, and beachfront property were not as much fun as a German castle with a mirror spy system and secret hiding room.

Today, the state of Connecticut is conserving one man's creative legacy. Some write, some paint, some sing, but William Gillette, even though he did write and act, expressed the inner workings of his mind in the architecture, the intricate woodwork, and the precise placement of stones of his palace. Gillette wrote in his will that he did not want a "blithing sap head" to inherit the land. He would be pleased to find out that the state has done an excellent job in preserving the land and the home just as it was when he dwelled in it, save for a newly added gift shop and a hotdog stand.

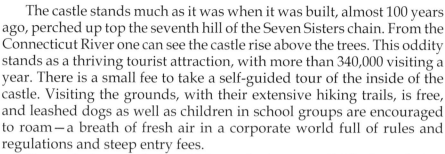

The castle stands much as it was when it was built, almost 100 years ago, perched up top the seventh hill of the Seven Sisters chain. From the Connecticut River one can see the castle rise above the trees. This oddity stands as a thriving tourist attraction, with more than 340,000 visiting a year. There is a small fee to take a self-guided tour of the inside of the castle. Visiting the grounds, with their extensive hiking trails, is free, and leashed dogs as well as children in school groups are encouraged to roam—a breath of fresh air in a corporate world full of rules and regulations and steep entry fees.

The park closes at dusk, which may be just as well. Workers closing up the castle have witnessed strange happenings, and some say that Gillette himself has not completely left.

The Castle is located just off Route 82 in East Haddam.

While You're There:

Essex Steam Train and Riverboat
Connecticut River Museum
Griswold Inn

Visit nearby Essex, home of the Essex Steam Train and Riverboat. The Riverboat actually passes right by Gillette Castle, as it travels along the Connecticut River. Essex, once voted best small town in America, has much to offer in terms of shopping, picturesque Colonial architecture, and the Connecticut River Museum.

My favorite Essex event happens every Monday night at the famed Griswold Inn. At that time, the banner outside The "Gris" proclaims "Sea Chanteys Tonight." The Jovial Crew, led by Connecticut's own Cliff Haslam, has performed there weekly for what seems like forever. The Jovial Crew performs traditional songs of the sea, as well as folk music of the British Isles. Cliff Haslam's CD *The Clockwinder*, available to buy during performances, was released in the 1980s on Sharon, Connecticut's Folk Legacy record label. *The Clockwinder* is a must-have recording for any traditional folk music fan. The Griswold Inn has been around since the dawn of this country, 1776. Various styles of live music are featured nightly at the taproom. The bar is situated in a circa 1735 school house that was added to the main building in 1801. The Gris is constantly heralded as the best bar in the state by *Connecticut Magazine*, and *Esquire* has called it one of the top 100 bars in the country. I almost forgot, the Griswold Inn is a working inn and features a top notch restaurant.

The Griswold Inn is located at 36 Main Street in Essex.

22.
Dinosaur State Park
Location: Rocky Hill

Located in an industrial park, right off busy Route 99 in the Hartford suburb of Rocky Hill, Dinosaur State Park is home to one of the biggest tracts of dinosaur tracks in the world. The complex includes a museum and woods with walking trails. The building where the museum is housed looks like a white turtle shell or an early bicycle helmet. Once inside the museum, the first attraction the visitor encounters is the gift shop. A popular place for dino-loving children, the museum has all kinds of toys, t-shirts, and trinkets that youngsters will beg to own. Although the museum is on the small side, the main attraction of the museum makes the trip worthwhile. In the center of the circular building is a huge slab of exposed rock. On these rocks are visible tracks of dinosaurs. A light demonstrates the path of each individual dinosaur as it traveled across the land. The footprints are remarkably well preserved and are easily and clearly seen. There are 500 tracks visible to the public and about three times more that are being preserved. Also in the museum is a diorama that depicts a scene, including a model dinosaur with a painted background of life during the Triassic period.

On August 23, 1966, while digging up rocky land off West Street in Rocky Hill in preparation for erecting a new State of Connecticut building, Edward McCarthy, the man operating the bulldozer, noticed something strange in the rock he was digging up. While excavating, he uncovered a large chunk of gray sandstone that had on it the fossilized imprint of six three-toed footprints. This caused quite a commotion, and soon scientists and state officials were brought in. Further digging uncovered a substantial number of tracks. The scientists and officials knew they were on to a great discovery! They needed to preserve their findings. The unearthing of this would lead to the eventual construction of the state park two years later. The excavations continued and hundreds of dinosaur tracks were found; these tracks remained untouched and now are the centerpiece of the museum, which is one of the biggest in the world.

Geologists and archeologists say that the Connecticut River Valley has long been a hotbed of dinosaur fossil findings. The tracks at the state park are called Eubrontes. Scientists believe that the dinosaur that caused these tracks was a meat eater, similar to the Dilophosaurus. A model of this dinosaur is the centerpiece of the diorama scene toward the back of the museum. The lengths of the tracks in the slab vary from ten to sixteen inches and are located 3.5 to 4.5 feet apart.

From the ticket booth and gift shop, the museum is set up in a circular fashion with walkways surrounding the tracks. In addition to the museum centerpiece, other fossils are found throughout the museum, including an extremely well-preserved "Otozoum" fossilized footprint.

The grounds also contain an arboretum, gardens, and two miles of preserved nature trails. A boardwalk helps visitors wind their way through the grounds. Since I'm no paleontologist, when I think of dinosaurs and dinosaur tracks, I envision the wild expanses of open land in southwestern United States. Dinosaur State Park is a neat tidbit of Connecticut (pre)history that awakens the inner scientist that is in all of us to the realization that these antediluvian creatures roamed wildly in the same locale where we now go about our daily routines. The park is also a great place to take the kids, especially when they are going through their "dinosaur stage."

> It's very reasonably priced ($6 for adults, free for children under 5 at the time of this writing), and it is a manageable size so that there will be no whines about tired feet and hungry stomachs. Dinosaur State Park is located on West Street, between Routes 3 and 99 in Rocky Hill, about a fifteen-minute drive south from Hartford on Interstate 91.

23.
National Submarine Memorial East and Submarine Force Museum and Library
Location: Groton

Eastern Connecticut is known mainly for three things: Mystic, casinos, and defense. Groton is home to both General Dynamics' Electric Boat facility and the Naval Submarine Base. In Connecticut lingo, these two are called "EB" and "The Sub Base." During the Cold War, both became huge places of employment for the workers of Eastern Connecticut. Although smaller in size today than during the Cold War years, these two places are still the top two employers in Groton.

Groton is known as the "submarine capital of the world," noted by the sign off of Route 95 entering Groton from New London across the Gold Star Bridge. Growing up in Eastern Connecticut, we were always told that after Washington, D.C. and New York City, Groton would be the third target of the Soviet nukes. Common questions were related to how far the blast would be felt and if my hometown of Norwich was in its radius. Luckily for all of us, the Soviet Union fell and Groton was left untouched. Now the biggest worry from Groton is the possible closing of the Base. Recently, during the Base Realignment and Closure process, the Submarine Base was on the list of those to be shut down, but due to petitions from local residents and politicians, the Base was allowed to remain open, at least for now.

The Conning Tower of the USS *Flasher* now stands tall as a monument to World War II fallen submarine victims. The Submarine Memorial is located in Groton.

The sub-curious visitor today can get up close and personal with a submarine. The Submarine Force Museum and Library is home to the decommissioned submarine the *USS Nautilus*, the first nuclear-powered submarine, which today is available for the public to explore. The museum depicts the vital role that Groton played in the defense of the United States during a crucial time in the country's history. The museum has tons of exhibits, informative for adults and interactive for children. The library portion includes thousands of documents, photos, and books related to submarines. While aboard the *Nautilus*, pretend you are a sailor, and you'll definitely find out whether you're claustrophobic!

Although the USS *Nautilus* and Submarine Force Library and Museum are not exactly off the beaten path nor that off-kilter, the role of the defense industry of Groton was an important and often overlooked part of American history. Speaking of overlooked, the Groton memorial to the submarine and to those who lost their lives on the undersea craft during World War II, is small and unpublicized compared to the aforementioned museum and library. Just like the museum, this memorial is free. And to the surprise of the unsuspecting passerby, a torpedo and the top chunk (conning tower) of a real submarine (the USS *Flasher*) is on display! Flanking the back section of the memorial is a Vietnam Memorial styled black-slab wall with the names of fallen submariners engraved on it. This wall is patterned after the front of a submarine that is heading down Groton's Thames River and out into the sea of the Long Island Sound. The monument is a nicely done remembrance of the Americans who lost their lives on the 52 submarines during World War II. In memorial to the fallen subs is a stone marker to commemorate each of them.

On my Memorial Day visit, I sat on a bench in the nicely manicured park-like area and contemplated the immensity of this submarine, as well as the immensity of the sacrifices made by our submariners in the service of their country.

> The World War II Submarine Memorial East is located at the corner of Bridge and Thames Street in Groton. Just look for the large conning tower. The Submarine Force Museum and Library is located at One Crystal Lake Road in Groton.

While You're There:

D'Elia's Bakery and Grinder Shop

Want more subs? How about the kind you can eat? About fifteen minutes up the road in Norwich is one of the best sub (or grinder) shops in the state. D'Elia's Bakery and Grinder Shop in downtown Norwich is a family-owned hole-in-the-wall that has been churning out superb sandwiches for many generations. Mainly a takeout place, the dimly lit interior is covered with religious pictures. Their sausage grinder could possibly be the world's greatest and their Italian and meatball grinders are not shabby, either. The bread, coupled with delicious meats and cheeses, is sublime.

> D'Elia's is located at 272 Franklin Street in Norwich.

24.
Connecticut's
Race Car Tracks
Locations: Thompson, Waterford, Lakeville, Stafford Springs

Get ready to start your engines! Welcome to the world of Connecticut Auto Racing. Auto racing is primarily associated with other parts of the country, namely the South and Midwest, but surprisingly, Connecticut has premier venues for the sport including professional NASCAR racetracks.

The Stafford Motor Speedway

The oldest racetrack is located in the northern part of the state, in the small town of Stafford Springs. The Stafford Motor Speedway, which was founded in 1870, welcomes a NASCAR series, as well as stock car and truck racing. Initially, the original kind of horsepower ruled this track; since the automobile was not yet invented, horses were doing the racing. Today, the competitors at Stafford Speedway battle for rank, as they zoom around the half-mile oval at ferocious speeds. The Stafford Springs Motor Speedway is located just off of Route 140 in Stafford Springs.

Thompson's International Speedway

The second oldest racetrack of the four is Thompson's International Speedway. Once known as the "Indianapolis of the East," this legendary track was initially built after the devastating Hurricane of '38, which left the town in a cloud of rubble. Today's speedway is much more than solely for racing; it includes a golf course and driving range. NASCAR stock car and modified cars are among the races that take place in Thompson.

The Speedway is located in the northeastern-most corner of the state, just off of Route 193 on East Thompson Road.

The Waterford Speedbowl

The Waterford Speedbowl, originally named the New London Speedbowl, first revved its engine in 1951 and has been wowing audiences ever since. This track is also home to NASCAR races, with a continuous emphasis on modified stock cars.

The Speedbowl is located on Route 85 in Waterford.

Lime Rock Park

The newest of the four parks is Lime Rock Park, located in the western part of the state, in the town of Lakeville. Lime Rock has seen a variety of competitors and vehicles grace its asphalt, from NASCAR-sanctioned stock cars and modified race cars, to Formula 1 racers and car shows featuring antique and classic automobiles. Lime Rock's most famous driver was actor Paul Newman who enjoyed racing cars along its one-and-a-half mile track.

Lime Rock is located just off of Route 112 in Lakeville.

All of the racetracks' seasons run during the warmer months.

These tracks offer more than just zooming drivers, but family events, car shows for the auto enthusiast, and public participation on certain occasions. The Demolition Derby is one of the most memorable events. I was the observer of not just a car demolition derby at the Waterford Speedbowl, but also to a school bus derby!

Friends of mine helped decorate a bus that they sponsored that was competing in said derby, so I decided to go. On this summer night, in the stands was a much younger set, with a high percentage of screaming elementary-aged children. The announcer prefaced the event with a taunt to the crowd aimed for this age dynamic, "Who here hates school buses?" Following this proclamation was a deafening roar from the stands. "Who hates school?" "YEAHHHH," yelled the kids. Similar exclamations from the announcer followed, which precipitated the buses smashing the rubber and metal out of one other. Luckily for us, the bus my friends painted a dastardly shade of convalescent home blue ended up victorious, the last bus that was in semi-workable condition.

The whole extravaganza lasted a few hours, including the car "burning rubber competition." (Ironically, I was a spectator to this the day after I watched Al Gore's *An Inconvenient Truth*.) Just as important, this was the only time I have seen a shrink-wrapped Cheese Whiz-stuffed green pepper, which was available for sale at the concession stand.

For all of you NASCAR and racing fans in general, Connecticut's an ideal place to "kick some asphalt!"

25.
Sculpturedale
Location: Kent

Interested in owning a new animal, but don't want the cleanup or have time for the care? Take a visit to Denis Curtiss's gallery called Sculpturedale in Kent. A retired world-traveling art teacher, Denis spends his time these days making metal animal sculptures. Ranging from small household pets, like dogs and cats, to large safari beasts, like giraffes and hippos, Denis fills almost any hankering for individual taste with a large variety of creatures. He also sculpts dancers and abstract figures. Sculpturedale features much of Curtiss's work; it's like walking through a safari park of metal animals. Sculpturedale is named for the Airdale Terrier rescue that cohabits his home and studio. His work can be seen in various places, including Andy Williams' Moon River Theater in Branson, Missouri, the AKC's Museum of Dog in St. Louis, and more locally, at the Interlaken Inn in nearby Lakeville, Connecticut.

Admission to Sculpturedale is free and is open on the weekends. Prices range from $2,000 to $10,000 per sculpture. Sculpturedale is located on Route 7.

While You're There:

Kent Falls State Park and Kent Falls
Next to Sculpturedale is Kent Falls State Park, one of Connecticut's biggest natural attractions. With picnicking grounds and the hiking trails, Kent Falls is a popular spot for families, outdoorsmen, and leaf peepers alike. The main attraction of Kent Falls is the waterfall; the series of waterfalls drop 250 feet in all, with the largest plummeting 70 feet.

Both Kent Falls is located on Route 7.

26.
Roadside Attractions

Locations: Dayville, Portland, Norwich, Uncasville, Montville, Hartford, Cheshire, Eastford, Preston, Waterbury, Norwalk, New Haven

Have you ever driven by an object of some kind, whether it be a giant bowling pin or prehistoric lizard, that has made you do a double-take? Connecticut has its share of head-turning roadside novelties.

The Big Cowboy

Starting our tour in Norwich takes us to two roadside attractions. In front of Surplus Unlimited, an odds-and-ends store in an otherwise nondescript strip mall, stands a twenty-four foot, giant fiberglass cowboy, who is often referred to as "The Big Cowboy" or, as my family called him when I was growing up, "Big Joe." The cowboy is actually a Muffler Man, which is a gigantic figure that is used to advertise something or someplace, often found in small towns. The cowboy stands guard, holding onto an American flag, dressed in blue jeans, a white shirt, and, of course, a cowboy hat. The figure once stood on the other side of Norwich in a warehouse owned by an eccentric treasure collector named Alix Cohn. The cowboy originally was utilized as an advertisement for a Phillips 66 gas station on West Town Street.

Connecticut is home to many roadside oddities and attractions, including two "Muffler Men" like this cowboy who stands in front of Surplus Unlimited Store in Norwich.

Bowling Pin

Also in Norwich, close to the site of the former Phillips 66 station, is a two-story-tall bowling pin. This roadside landmark denotes the locale of Norwich Bowling and Entertainment Center. Hey, you can still pick up the spare! Both of these odd attractions have been featured in Zippy comics.

A Second Muffler Man

The state is luckily home to two Muffler Men. The other is located outside the House of Doors on West Johnson Avenue in Cheshire. This

Muffler Man is styled as Paul Bunyan and, just like the cowboy, he is a flag-waving patriot.

Dog and Frog

Two animals that really rock are located in the eastern part of the state. Dog Rock shows a spotted mug of a stony black and white pooch located on Route 165 in Preston. Another rocky animal is Frog Rock in Eastford. This stone-faced, green-painted amphibian is located on Route 44. For four times the number of slippery fellows, perched upon spools of twine, visit Willimantic's Frog Bridge, located on Route 32 on the bridge across the Willimantic River. See Chapter 17 for more detail.

E-A-T

A classic highway-side sign that tells drivers to E-A-T is for Zip's Diner at Exit 93 on 395 in the Dayville section of Killingly. Established in 1954, the focal point of the retro diner includes a metal tower rising high above the restaurant spelling out the simple three-letter invitation. The classic diner fare here includes bottomless coffee, breakfast served all day, and such staples as Yankee Pot Roast. Additionally, Zip's serves a few offbeat choices, such as the Southern favorite, chicken fried steak!

Wells Dinosaur Haven

The fossils discovered at Rocky Hill must have caused quite a prehistoric stir in the Nutmeg State. In Portland, there is a dino-themed mini golf, full of Jurassic obstacles. In Uncasville on Route 32, a T-Rex proudly frightens would-be home invaders away with its smiling grin. This is Wells Dinosaur Haven, containing several handmade dinosaurs that you can visit for free—just call ahead.

Dinosaur Place and Nature's Art

Also, in the small town of Montville is "Dinosaur Place and Nature's Art," which contains a museum, store, and park wrapped up all into one. Making its presence felt is the large Tyrannosaur welcoming visitors. He dresses up for summertime, Christmas, and other holiday celebrations. During Christmas, he wears a Santa cap upon his large, flat head. The walking trails in the back of Nature's Art are strewn with other life-sized dinosaurs.

The Dinosaur Place at Nature's Art is located on Route 85 in the Oakdale section of Montville.

Samuel Colt Armory and The Christmas House

Although Hartford is known for such beautiful architecture as the state capitol and the double-turreted, medieval style of the Soldiers and Sailors Monument, another of the most recognizable of Hartford's great buildings is the Samuel Colt Armory. Its most memorable feature is undoubtedly its blue onion dome reminiscent of a Russian Orthodox Church. Driving south from downtown Hartford on Interstate 91 gives the driver a superb view. In New Britain, across from the worthwhile New Britain Museum of Art, is the Christmas House. A private residence, the halls get more than a little decked during the "most wonderful time of the year."

The Christmas House is available for in-house visits during certain seasonal evenings.

Stew Leonards

Stop by the original Stew Leonards gigantic grocery store on Route 1 in Norwalk for a mooing good time. In addition to literally tons of food, there are talking cows, a singing dairy product rock band, a bovine trapeze artist, and during December, a whole lot of holiday cheer. Go for the food, stay for the entertainment, make sure you bring a grocery list because otherwise it is easy to forget what you originally came in for!

Pirelli Building

Also mentioned in another chapter, Waterbury's Holy Land's cross can be seen atop Slocum Hill, looming over the Brass City. Although not kitschy like a gigantic hot dog or ball of twine, New Haven is home to the Pirelli Building, which looks more like a large concrete Lego block on top of a smaller concrete Lego block that is being held up on both sides by two concrete supports. Between the two supports is a gaping hole, making this currently vacant building truly unique, if not truly ugly. The Pirelli Building is located next to IKEA in the western part of the city, in its Long Wharf District. Interstate 95 southbound offers a perfect view of the Pirelli Building; often traffic is creeping along or at a standstill near this location, giving passersby the opportunity to take a long look at this example of modern architecture.

Section 4: Events

The Yantic Falls is the location of the famous "Indian Leap."

1.
Connecticut's Outposts of Little People
Locations: Norwich, Middlebury, Bridgeport, Willimantic, Canaan

My late grandmother, Elizabeth "Gaggi" Lalla, was raised and spent the majority of her years living on Plain Hill Road in the Bean Hill section of Norwich. As a young girl, her father owned a small farm consisting of a few acres. Gaggi was a storyteller, and she would repeat the same tale over and over again, as we passed by certain points on the way to such places as church, the store, or different exits off the highway. On our annual trip to Pennsylvania, as we passed the exit for Newtown, Connecticut, she would regale us with the story of a man who had a unique method of disposing of his deceased wife's body. You know in that town, a few years ago, a man put his wife through a wood chipper.

Little Men

No more or less detail than that, but alas, the same story. In her succinct style, Gaggi often repeated a story of her childhood. Around age eight, making it the year 1925, Gaggi was playing behind her house, in the woods near a stream. Although the story was not chock-full of vivid details, it still was certainly entertaining, for she clearly stated that she was witness to "little men" hopping and dancing about in the grass and on top of anthills. These mini-humans were adorned in typical gnome fashion, with pointy hats and beards, resembling storybook elves. She believed her words completely, as she claimed to have seen them on more than one occasion. Whereas ghost stories or tales of unusual beasts made my elementary-aged mind race and goose bumps form on my arms, the little people story to me was nothing but fantasy.

Since this story lacked detail and could not lead to further investigation, I struggled as I may, but felt that it was not appropriate to add to this collection. Reading Joseph Citro's *Passing Strange*, a superb collection of New England supernatural tales and legends, made me feel otherwise. In a section of the book that described the presence of little people throughout New England, part of a chapter was dedicated to what local Native Americans referred to as Makiawisag, or in essence, *little people*. The story goes that Martha Uncas, a younger relative of the Mohegan Sachem, Uncas, was paddling down the Yantic River with her family and saw the Makiawisag running alongside the shore. Her mother told her not to look at the dwarfs for they would become invisible. When invisible, these little people would cause much mischief. Martha's mother further warned her that if the elves appeared at your doorstep and asked for food, you'd better comply. If you didn't provide them with some grub, they would point their finger at you, become invisible, and enter the house to take far more than originally requested.

It's a rather strange coincidence that in both stories the little people are in close proximity to the Yantic River. The Yantic is a small river beginning near Colchester and ending in the Norwich harbor. Gaggi's visits with the little men occurred in the Bean Hill section of Norwich, not far from the Yantic River, where Martha's little men also scampered. Strange as this coincidence was, and although there was no mention of Norwich or Bean Hill in the passage, it was captivating. Although neither story is filled with elaborate detail, the locations of both add to the intrigue.

Old Men of the Mountains

A similar tale exists from the opposite corner of the state in the town of Canaan. These comparable elves were called "old men of the mountains" dressed in long gray robes. They often avoided contact with their regular-sized counterparts, but when they did, the elves affected the humans' senses and made them feel not themselves. Be prepared to be robbed by them if you did not pay their tithes. If you do oblige their requests, you may be rewarded with triangular coins with distinctive markings on them. This is reminiscent of Washington Irving's tale "Rip Van Winkle," taking place in the Catskills, not far from Canaan. Rip, in his desire to escape his shrewish wife, takes a hike in the mountains where he comes upon a little man who takes him to visit a group of very odd fellows, all playing ninepin and drinking copiously. When Rip sneaks some sips, he becomes very sleepy, and when he wakes up, twenty years have passed. This tale's ending is happy, however, with Rip's miserable wife now dead and his companion, a dog, still alive. He has missed the horrors of war, with the American Revolution, and spends the rest of his days spinning yarns in the tavern.

Little People Village

Middlebury, a town on the direct opposite side of the state, is home to one of the state's most popular family attractions, Quassy Amusement Park. It is also the location of the Little People Village. Located off of

Route 63, there remains a crumbling village of three- to four-foot houses, some with pinpointed detail like staircases and stories. Legend goes that this property belonged to a husband and wife. The wife frequently saw little folk—some kind of fairies, small demons, or devils. The wife requested that her husband create a village of houses for these little people. From here, the stories veer off.

Also on the property is a human-sized throne that the husband built for his wife, the "Queen of the Little People." One tale says that the husband killed his wife because he was tired of her insanity and her bossing him around, and then killed himself. The other version goes that the wife was going to kill her husband because he wanted to sit on her throne, but the little demons got rid of her first.

Today, the throne remains, but brings bad luck to all who sit on it—really bad luck. Such bad luck that whoever sits on the throne will die in a short period of time. Others say that the location is still swarming with the little demons, and some swear that the husband and wife also haunt the grounds. Some visitors to the location have been driven insane, just like the Queen. Other investigators claim the area as simply having negative energy.

In reality, these dwellings suitable for a doll were once part of nearby Quassy's "Fairy Village." Quassy Amusement Park was founded in 1908, the same year that a trolley line was installed from Waterbury to Middlebury. After World War II, Quassy became the amusement park that we know today. The Fairy Village ceased existence once the trolley extension from Quassy's main park was discontinued. The Fairy Village was built in the 1920s, but even to visitors back then, it seemed in a constant state of disrepair; it was never kept up as it should have been.

One of the state's biggest, or should I say smallest, celebrities was an actual little person, General Tom Thumb, who, at his tallest, reached three-feet, four-inches, at the time of his death in 1883. Promoted by the state's premier entrepreneur and entertainer, P.T. Barnum discovered Tom when he was only a child. Barnum showcased unusual human beings, negatively called "freaks." Born Charles Sherwood Stratton in Bridgeport in 1838, General Tom Thumb was the only small person in his otherwise normally sized family. He married another small person, named Lavinia Warren and became quite wealthy, owning homes in New York City and on the reclusive celebrity retreat, Branford's Thimble Islands. At the time of his death, Barnum had created a life- sized statue of Tom Thumb to mark his grave. He is buried at Mt. Grace Cemetery in Bridgeport.

For more information on the life of P.T. Barnum and General Tom Thumb, visit the Barnum Museum in Bridgeport.

Barnum Museum

After severe damage from a "freak" tornado, the Barnum Museum closed for reconstruction in 2010. This delightful museum, appealing to all ages, has recently reopened for two days each week, and the refurbishing is ongoing. Bridgeport is also the location of a P.T. Barnum statue.

Midget Town

Another tale that was spun in Eastern Connecticut comes from the Willimantic Camp Meeting located on Route 32 in Windham. This enclave of tiny gingerbread cottages was created as a Methodist retreat center, popular at the time of its founding, 1860. Looking like a tired brother to the grand camp meeting grounds at Oak Bluffs on Martha's Vineyard, this cluster of about 100 small buildings was nicknamed "Midget Town." Although extremely politically incorrect, the gist was that it was a private sanctuary for the area's little people. The "No Trespassing" signs were off-putting as well.

On my first trip through the village, a few friends and I parked down the street at the IGA grocery store and walked uphill to the entrance. By foot, we only explored about a quarter of the village and saw no signs of anyone. Getting more courageous, we took the car up to investigate further. As the car meandered through the series of one-way streets, we saw normal-sized people, which dispelled the myth of Midget Town. Nevertheless, it was a different kind of place. The cottages stood in different stages of habitation, some looking like the house that Jack built, and others so perfectly picturesque that you would expect Hansel and Gretel to come knocking. Along with the numerous cottages, signs kept pointing to the "Victoria House," which turned out to be the administration building of sorts, with a community function room.

I visited the Camp Meeting on a few occasions, mostly to revel in the marked difference of these homes and setting to the surrounding town. One time, during a very early morning car ride, delivering newspapers with a friend, I really got to examine the Camp Meeting more closely. Instead of rolling by the houses, we had to stop to deliver the *Willimantic Chronicle* to the many subscribers in the village. By this time, I had become a frequent visitor to Martha's Vineyard and was familiar with the gingerbread houses of Oak Bluffs and knew their religious significance.

The houses were used primarily as summer cottages for the individuals in different parishes of the Methodist Church. Similar in style, these serve the same function.

Today, these cottages contain some residents that stay year-round and others only for the summer. The cottage enclave still serves the purpose of prayer and overall rejoicing in God. Services continue to be held in the summertime. In addition to the cottages and Victoria House, there is a function hall, library, and Ladies Improvement Society. The cottage decoration ranges from brightly colored and elaborate to drab and shabby. The wooden cottages are so tiny (smaller than their Oak Bluffs counterparts) that it is no wonder that the myth of smaller people living in them arose. The majority of the cottages were built between 1868 and 1877; there were three times as many houses then as there are today thanks to the demolition caused by the Hurricane of '38.

For the curious visitor, please be respectful of the residents as you drive or walk around the village. This is ultimately a religious place. The Camp Meeting is located on the left-hand side of Route 32 before entering downtown Willimantic from the south.

After all this, my grandmother was right; I now understand why people say Connecticut is a "little" state!

2.
Offbeat Connecticutians
Locations: Norwich, Waterbury, Old Lyme

A bulk of the chapters in this collection have to do with places of notoriety. This chapter is different; it is less about place and more about the individual who made his or her mark on the Nutmeg State.

Ellis Ruley

Ellis Ruley's work today can be seen in prominent museums and galleries throughout the United States, including Hartford's Wadsworth Athaneum (America's oldest public art museum), New York's Museum of American Folk Art, and Washington, D.C.'s Corcoran Gallery. His brand of folk art was not always so highly touted, though. Ruley, a Norwich native, lived in the Laurel Hill section of the city in the first half of the twentieth century. A construction worker by trade, Ruley spent countless hours honing his brand of folk art which featured colorful scenes depicted with house paint on cardboard. Ruley's images contained cartoonish animals and people.

He was inspired by nature around him as well as magazine images, rendering both to his artistic vision. Pieces like "Garden of Eden" have made Ruley a folk art legend. Murder and mystery play into the Ruley story. In 1948, his son–in–law was found dead in a well, and Ruley himself was found dead, eleven years later, on his land, frozen, with a gash in his forehead. No one was convicted of either murder, and officially no foul play was detected in Ruley's death, but friends and relatives believe otherwise.

Ruley had a large tract of land on Laurel Hill, which was an envy of his neighbors. His wife and he were also the first interracial couple in Norwich, and this did not sit well with some other townspeople. Six months after Ruley's death, his house mysteriously burned down with his paintings inside. Sadly, Ruley was never able to experience his fame during his lifetime.

Tommy Macaione

Another painter with eastern Connecticut ties is renowned Santa Fe artist, Tommy Macaione. Macaione was born in New London and worked in Norwich as a barber. Habitually bad at keeping appointments, Macaione was fired almost daily by his boss, my grandfather Joe Lalla, but rehired just the same. Tommy would threaten that "one day I'll hitch a ride to Phoenix."

One day in 1952, Tommy made true his threat, when he found his way to the Southwestern U.S., not to Phoenix, but instead to Santa Fe. During his tenure in Santa Fe, he went on to become a colorful figure who was known for making brightly colored paintings, reminiscent of Monet and Van Gogh. He owned a slew of cats and dogs, at one point numbering 85, and even ran for mayor. Nicknamed "El Diferente," Tommy was featured as a tour guide in a 1961 version of the Santa Fe tourism brochure. Macaione passed away in 1992, but his legacy lives on in the city where a park features a bronze statue of him in mid-painting, with a beloved dog by his side. Tommy didn't make much money in his lifetime; often he traded his art for dog food to keep his companions going. Macaione's work today fetches a price tag in the thousands and is figured prominently in places like Santa Fe City Hall. New London's Lyman Allyn Art Museum also featured an extensive exhibit of his work. Pretty good work from an eccentric barber from New London!

The Nut Lady

Traveling down to the coast, Old Lyme was once home to the famed Nut Museum, the creation of Elizabeth Tashjian, the proclaimed Nut Lady. Featured on television shows like *Late Night with David Letterman*, Tashjian created a shrine to her beloved nut. The Nut Museum was located in an Old Lyme mansion and was fashioned with everything nut, from nut artwork to nutcrackers to nut music and, of course, actual nuts. A high point was the thirty-five-pound, coco-de-mer nut. Elizabeth took visitors on a tour of her museum and ended the tour with a rendition of her song "Nuts are Beautiful."

Admission to the museum was a few bucks and a nut. The Nut Museum was in existence for about thirty years, but ultimately trouble between Tashjian and the town resulted in the museum's closure and the house being put up for sale while she was in a coma. Tashjian passed away in 2007, but the collection was thankfully bought by Connecticut College in nearby New London and has been displayed at the Lyman Allyn Museum.

Salvatore Verdirome

Another curious attraction or actually former attraction in the same vein as Holy Land, discussed in another chapter, was the Sanctuary of Love, in Norwich. In 1971, Salvatore Verdirome decided that he should turn his sloped backyard into a shrine for the Virgin Mary and saints. The idea came to him while he was working at Electric Boat in Groton as a carpenter — he was struck by a vision of the Virgin Mary. The vision directed him to create a holy shrine. This was not any ordinary shrine with marble or stone, but instead Verdirome's creation was made of materials similar to those of Holy Land.

The Sanctuary of Love, taken down by the city in 2002, was located on Route 12 in Norwich on North Main Street. The houses on this part of the street overlook the Shetucket River and have properties that include a steep hillside slope, which made a perfect canvas for Verdirome's masterpiece. The statues, which counted around fifty, were placed inside old-fashioned clawfoot bathtubs painted blue, which provided a shell for the figures they were covering. Displays commemorated biblical events such as the Ten Commandments, Jesus's nativity, and the Crucifixion. Verdirome also created the Sea of Glass, from the Revelations chapter of the Bible, made from glass supplied by the nearby Thermos Factory. Christmas lights helped illuminate the hillside land. With a sign that read "Your faith brought you here" out front, the Sanctuary was a popular stop for gamblers en route to either casino hoping to have good luck or to make amends due to the guilt for the money they would gamble away.

Sadly, the house was condemned, due to a massive unpaid tax bill, which eventually led to the displacement of Verdirome and an eventual disassembly of the Sanctuary by the town. Verdirome passed away in 2004.

The Sanctuary of Love is closely related to Waterbury's Holy Land, not only in the religious theme, but also in the vision that the builders had. Both men had the goal of educating the masses by creating testaments to their Christianity. Throughout the country and the world, other cities have also been built by motivation of a vision or a call from God, like the Watts Towers in Los Angeles and the Ave Maria Grotto in Alabama.

Each of these Connecticutians had a different story to tell, all unique, but similarly creating a fabric of individuality and folk culture. Although they have all passed on, they each leave a legacy that will not be forgotten.

3.
Three Tales of Yankee Connecticut
Locations: Norwich and Bozrah

The idea of the Connecticut Yankee, made famous by Mark Twain, had certain intrinsic values and traits, some of which are thriftiness, piousness, and a curmudgeonly attitude. Stories of the hard-nosed New Englander, trekking in the snow by foot to the market, using a wood stove, and wearing a jacket inside instead of turning the heat on, are common Yankee depictions. The Norwich region has three classic stories of Yankees who were uncompromising, one even after his death.

Mr. M Comes Back

The houses in the Jail Hill section of Norwich sit high atop the city below and have a pristine view of the once-bustling harbor. The name comes from the old city jail that was located there. In the early 1900s, there lived a man and his wife. The wife was a quiet, reserved, caring woman who will be referred to as Mrs. M. for privacy's sake. Her husband, Mr. M., could not be described in the same way. He was a miser, a cantankerous fellow who was constantly unpleasant and who even hid his money under the floorboards of his house. The years went on, and the old man died. The scrooge was so stingy that he wanted to take his money with him in the next life. Not satisfied with a penniless death, Mr. M. came back to get it!

Soon after he passed on, dishes in the house were smashed, furniture was moved, and altogether chaos ensued. Was it an intruder? The problems persisted, as wallpaper was torn off the wall. Mrs. M. wanted to remedy this, but her prayers were not helping. She hired the assistance of a local priest who blessed the house. By then there was speculation that Old Man M. was the cause of the bedlam. The priest told the ghost of Mr. M. to leave the house alone, that he could not take earthly possessions with him (wherever he was going).

Mr. M. did not want to hear this, and he continued to haunt his old home. The priest told Mrs. M. to change the house around so that Old Man M. would not recognize his former abode. She re-wallpapered, painted the ceilings, and finally the priest blessed the home once again. This time, Mr. M. did not come back. So even in the afterlife, a Connecticut Yankee does not want to part with his money.

The Jail Hill section of Norwich is located atop School Street near the downtown.

Just the Right Dinner?

The story of Mr. T takes place in the Fitchville section of Bozrah, which is the main village of the town, in an old farmhouse located about a mile from the town center. A Yankee tradition was to eat beans on Saturday nights; hence the popularity still today of bean suppers at local churches in New England. A section of Norwich is even called Bean Hill, which was named after the prized legume. In the early twentieth century, Farmer T was eating his bean dinner on a Saturday night, when his house was broken into and he was slain. He had apparently been stabbed to death, with blood streaks on the walls. When the police went to investigate the crime scene, there was no body to be found. A while later, a skeleton was found off of Sandy Desert Lane, on the Montville-Norwich line (today an entrance to the Mohegan Sun casino), which some people thought was the remains of Mr. T. Later, when it was found that the skeleton was not Mr. T, the search continued, but the case was never solved.

A local family had a farm and butchered their own pigs to sell to the local markets. The pig meat was popular in town, best tasting cuts in the region, maybe it was because of what the pigs were consuming? Unbeknownst to the reason why, sources close to the family hinted that Old Man T's body was ground up and used as food for the piggies. Now that's good eating!

Today, Mr. T's house is located at Exit 24 off Route 2.

Jane Maria Johnson

In the tradition of classic folktales, or Native American legends, this story varies a bit based on whom you talk to. This is the story of the ill-fated Jane Maria Johnson of Bozrah, the daughter of a prominent and wealthy doctor in town. In the mid-1800s, at 26 and unwed, Jane was already considered an old maid. Her suitor, William Irving, was an Irishman who worked as a gardener on her family's estate. One variation of the tale has William and Jane as lovers who realized that their love affair could not continue in the social society that existed in Victorian Bozrah. Another variation has Mr. Irving pursuing Miss Johnson and she rejecting his advances. Either way, the story ends with Jane killed from a bludgeoning from the butt of a gun by William, and William with a self-inflicted razor blade slit from ear to ear. Jane was buried underneath a stone with only her name etched upon it in the family plot in the Bozrah Rural Cemetery. William, on the other hand, is also buried in the same cemetery, but his headstone is slanted at a crazy angle with words on the stone detailing his crime. His special post-mortem treatment was to be buried standing on his head so that he could never achieve eternal rest for the heinous deed he had committed.

Bozrah native-son Richard Magni remembers hearing a much different variant of this tale. As a child in the local school, and learning of legends of the town, the story he shared did not include William Irving. Jane Maria, again an old maid at 26, in this version fell in love with and slept with a married man. When Jane died, she was the one buried upside down so that she could not rest peacefully after committing a mortal sin.

So either way, legend has it that there is someone buried standing on their head at the Bozrah Rural Cemetery.

On a recent visit to the cemetery, I was able to locate the graves of the Johnson family, including Jane's marker with only her name inscribed on it. After much scouring of the grounds, I was left empty-handed, since I was not able to locate William Irving's gravestone. Some believers in the first rendition say that Irving was never buried in the cemetery, but instead, his body was quickly donated to science.

The grave of Samuel Johnson w daughter, as legend has it, was murdered in the town of Bozra

Bozrah Rural Cemetery is located on Schwartz Road in Bozrah, not far off Exit 23 of Route 2.

Today, there are two cemeteries joined together: Bozrah Rural and Johnson Cemetery. The latter is still an active burying ground for citizens. The Johnson family plot is located near the front of Bozrah Rural; when facing the gate, it is towards the left.

Another interesting feature in the cemetery is the Potter's Field located near the back of the first cemetery. A Potter's Field is an area where unknown people are buried without any kind of markers.

These three tales of the Connecticut Yankee hone in on traits often associated with the "typical" Yankee persona: curmudgeonly Mr. M., so thrifty with his money that he came back from the dead to get it; Mr. T., who was murdered while eating beans on a Saturday night in true Yankee fashion; and lastly, Jane Maria, whose family buried her on her head to secure eternal unrest for committing an unpardonable sin!

4.
Witchcraft in Connecticut
Locations: Hartford, Wethersfield, Fairfield, Stratford, Groton

Witchcraft in New England, or even in America, is dominated by the Salem Witch Trials of Massachusetts, with no mention of the witch accusations in other states. Although Salem took the lion's share of witch finger pointing and execution, witches were tried and killed in other colonies including Virginia, New York, and Connecticut. Salem, whose trials were resurrected in the Arthur Miller play *The Crucible*, has embraced its dark past by promoting numerous witch-themed tourist attractions. Connecticut keeps its witches in the closet.

The most famous Connecticut witch was Goody Bassett of Stratford who was hanged in May 1651. Witches were being tried and executed in Connecticut about 50 years before the Salem Witch Trials of 1692. Goody Bassett was said to have been conjured by Eliakim Phelps, who owned a mansion in Stratford in the mid-1800s. The Phelps Mansion was one of the most haunted places in the state, but was torn down in the 1970s. Connecticut witch accusations were rampant in Hartford, Wethersfield, and Fairfield. For example, Ann Cole from Hartford was said to have her words and tongue controlled by demons, for she was saying things that were not her own. In the Hartford area alone, about ten people were condemned for witchery, with four of them being executed.

Although Connecticut's witching past may not live in infamy as its northerly neighbor's does, the accusations and executions of innocent victims still casts an undesirable shadow on the Nutmeg State.

5.
Tales of Pirate Treasure
Location: Milford

When thinking about the state of Connecticut in a historical perspective, most people would reference Colonial New England, the Victorian Era, or pre-colonial Native American settlements. Not many would think of pirates. On the contrary, Connecticut has its share of pirate legends, the most famous being tales of the infamous buccaneer, Captain Kidd. In 1699, near the end of Kidd's pirating career, he was sailing from New York to Boston and is said to have buried his treasure along the way.

One of the most popular beaches in Connecticut today is Silver Sands State Park in Milford, and with good reason. Silver Sands is one of the very few free public beaches in the state. Only a short drive from congested Route 1, Silver Sands seems miles away. It is equipped with a picnic area and a long boardwalk that goes from the parking lot to the beach and also cuts through tidal marshland, home to many species of nesting birds like terns and egrets. The beach and state park area was formerly a town landfill.

Other than a place for a pleasant family outing in the summer, Silver Sands also has an unusual reputation. When looking out into Long Island Sound from the beach, one can see Charles Island, the large piece of land directly across from Silver Sands. This island is home to otherworldly legends. Charles Island is about a half mile into the Sound from the beach. At low tide, a tombolo, or generally speaking, a sandbar, connects the island to the main land. Beachgoers can walk on this tombolo, but beware, the tide comes in fast! They cannot, however, walk on the land of the island, for today it is a wildlife refuge and is not accessible to the public during the birds' nesting season.

Legend says that Captain Kidd may have buried his treasure in different locales throughout Long Island Sound. A factual account says that he did bury treasure on Gardner's Island, which is part of Long Island, but it was later found and dug up. Other accounts have Kidd burying the treasure in Norwalk, the Thimble Islands in Branford, and most notably, on Charles Island in Milford. Some say this island was cursed by Kidd and by others who spent time here including local Native Americans. There are tales of treasure-seekers finding more than they bargained for. Two unlucky men looking for the treasure found it, along with a severed whistling head. Severely frightened, they rushed back to land, and when they returned the next day, the treasure (along with the whistling head) was gone.

The island has never been able to house a permanent settlement — another reason why it is considered cursed. Some people say they have seen glowing lights in its woods. In the 1930s, the island was home to a monastery and religious retreat. So whoever, or whatever, is making a commotion on the island, be it treasure, a curse from a Native American, from Captain Kidd, or an otherworldly remnant of the religious retreat, Charles Island certainly has notoriety.

Other than the paranormal allure, Charles Island and Silver Sands State Park has an expanse of picturesque beach looking out on the waters of Long Island Sound (and again, it is free!). A great place for a picnic, and a day at the beach, tell the kids to bring the pails and shovels, for they may just find more than seawater at the bottom of the hole.

Silver Sands State Park is off Route 1 in Milford on Silver Sands Park Way.

6.
Indian Leap
Location: Norwich

The Native American legend is a popular type of folktale. New England has its share of these, since many Native American tribes once populated the land, from the northern tip of Maine to the current bedroom towns of New York. Eastern Connecticut was inhabited by three major tribes: the Narragansett, the Mohegan, and the Pequot. In 1644, after a long series of battles and treaties between the tribes of Eastern Connecticut and the European settlers, the Narragansett and the Mohegan waged war on one another.

The story goes that the Narragansett were winning the war, when Uncas, the Mohegan sachem, asked to meet Miantonomo, the sachem of the Narragansett, face-to-face. He complied, and when asked to fight man to man, the Narragansett leader said *no*. Uncas then threw himself on the ground, which was a signal for the Mohegan braves to attack. The surprised Narragansett had to retreat.

This confrontation was said to happen on the Great Plain in Norwich, Connecticut, near the present Route 82. The retreating tribe, who were on Mohegan territory, split in two and took two different ways back home. Miantonomo led his group over the Yantic River at the Yantic Falls. With the Mohegan close on their tail, the Narragansett sachem made a daring escape, jumping across the falls, although many of his men plummeted to a painful death on jagged rocks some fifty feet below.

The legend holds that Uncas leapt over the falls as if he were flying. Soon enough, he caught up with Miantonomo. Uncas eventually captured the chief of the Narragansett and brought him to the central part of the Mohegan territory. The Mohegan leaders pondered for a long while over what to do with the sachem, and eventually decided to execute him near the spot where he was captured. Uncas took Miantonomo a few miles away from the falls to what is now the Greenville section of Norwich. He killed Miantonomo, and then cut and ate part of his shoulder out of respect for the fallen enemy leader. In the mid-nineteenth century, a granite monument was erected for the Narragansett leader. Before that, only a pile of stones marked his final resting place.

In a historical account of the Narragansett/Mohegan War, there is no mention of Uncas leaping over the Yantic Falls. According to that account, in the 1640s, the Narragansett waged war on the Mohegan after siding with them in the Pequot war, which almost wiped out that tribe entirely. Since the Mohegan were closely knit with the English colonists, the Narragansett were not happy with Uncas's and the tribe's steady increase in power. The Mohegan were losing the battle against the attacking Narragansett when Uncas captured their leader, Miantonomo, near Shetucket, the Mohegan center of operation (present-day Norwich). It seems that since the Mohegan were the only tribe left in Eastern Connecticut, they were allowed to embellish the story of their victory however they pleased.

In an account from Narragansett history, again there was no mention of Uncas leaping over the waterfall, but instead the story goes that Miantonomo was captured at the Yantic Falls, and some of his warriors fell off the ledge, but neither sachem leaped over it.

It seems that the basic facts were correct; the outnumbered Uncas and his battalion captured Miantonomo in Norwich, later to kill him in Greenville, and have the tides of war change in Uncas's favor. Like Napoleon writing his own accounts of his battles, making treacherous journeys and fights look glorious, Uncas most likely did the same thing. As the story was passed on from one generation to the next, fabrications and embellishments increased. Although in reality, the jump never occurred, the popular legend relates that Uncas did in fact jump over the Yantic Falls, henceforth giving it the nickname "Indian Leap," what locals still call it today.

The Royal Mohegan Burial Ground is located up the hill on Sachem Street, which is the final resting place of Uncas. Andrew Jackson presided over the ceremony for Uncas's monument. Much of the Royal Mohegan Burial Ground did not receive the same respect as Uncas. A good portion of the land between Yantic Falls and the nearby town common called Chelsea Parade is part of the burial ground, although it is not labeled. To make room for the adjoining neighborhood, bodies were dug up and burned. During the construction of the Masonic Temple, bodies were discovered, but ignored and construction continued. The Temple was razed in 2006. Today a memorial park is located on the former Masonic Temple land.

This location, officially known as Yantic Falls, is nicknamed "Indian Leap" due to the Native American legends associated with this spot.

Indian Leap is a lovely place to visit any time of year. The roaring falls can be viewed from a small bridge across the river. At the bottom of the hill is a refurbished factory building, now housing apartments and condos. This marks the beginning of the Heritage Riverfront Walkway, which follows the river to the harbor in downtown Norwich.

Indian Leap is located just off Route 2, on Sachem Street in Norwich, which is also the location of the Royal Mohegan Burial Ground. The Miantonomo Monument is also in Norwich, in the Greenville section of the town. Take Route 12 in Norwich and look for the large green side that reads "Miantonomo Monument."

7.
The Last Wolf in Connecticut?
Locations: Pomfret, Brooklyn, Ledyard/Stonington

Israel Putnam, along with Nathan Hale, is considered one of the state's heroes. Although known in his later life for daring war feats and impossible escapes from capture, as a young man his execution of Connecticut's last wolf was the event that made him legendary.

Putnam, although born in Danvers, Massachusetts, moved in his early twenties to his beloved Connecticut, where numerous landmarks would eventually bear his name, including Putnam State Park in Redding, the town of Putnam, and many Putnam Streets. At age 21, along with his wife and children, he moved to the town of Mortlake, which was once part of Pomfret. (Later this section would break off from Pomfret and rename itself Brooklyn.)

During the winter of 1742-1743, something ravaged Putnam's sheep and goats, killing seventy of them. The same menace had attacked neighbors' livestock as well. Seeing tracks in the snow led Putnam to decipher what killed his animals—it was a wolf! Not just any wolf though, a wolf that only had three toes on one paw. This was the same elusive wolf that had been terrorizing the region's farm animals for years. Putnam was extremely peeved and needed to put an end to this.

Putnam and a few neighbors tracked the she-wolf for hours, until eventually the lead tracker followed the beast into a cave about three miles from Putnam's Mortlake house. The band of yeomen tried all they could to lure the creature out of the den. They tried to smoke the wolf out and even brought a hound into the den to face the wolf. The hound did not fare so well, as it came out badly scratched. Israel Putnam decided to have a showdown with the wolf himself. He crawled into the den with musket and torch in hand. The musket blast left the wolf lifeless. Once Putnam knew the wolf was dead, he grabbed it. His neighbors pulled him out of the den along with wolf, musket, and torch in tow. Putnam brought the wolf to a local tavern where it was hung up for the public to see. Farmers from all over the county made pilgrimages to rejoice at the sight of the departed beast that had been a menace to their farms and their livelihoods.

Putnam went on to be revered with mythological status in his home state. After many tumultuous years as a high-ranking officer in the army, and often facing down death, he passed on in 1790. He was buried at a cemetery in Brooklyn, but had to be removed due to hero worshippers frequenting and causing wear to his grave. His body spent time in Hartford, but eventually found a final resting place underneath the monument dedicated to him located in the center of Brooklyn. On each side of the Putnam statue's base are two wolf heads, representing his execution of Connecticut's final wolf.

So Putnam's encounter lay to rest the final wolf — end of story. Well, not quite. The wolf had always been an integral part of the state's history, including being the name of a prominent Native American tribe, the Mohegan. The Mohegan name is derived from an indigenous word meaning *wolf*. In copious towns across the state, many street names include the word "wolf," but officially according to the State of Connecticut, there are no more wolves in the state.

I beg to differ at this statement. Unlike most chapters in this book, I have not been a witness firsthand to any supernatural event, but I have seen wolves in the state, twice. Driving on the back woods near the Ledyard/Stonington border, close to Foxwoods Resort Casino, on Lantern Hill Road in the Fall of 2009, I spotted what I truly believe to be wolves. A quiet dark street with no lights, I drove past Abbey's Lantern Hill Inn, and soon after, saw what looked like dogs in the street. I approached cautiously in fear of hitting the animals, and also in hopes that the animals had dog tags and I could help them find their way back home. As I got closer, the "dogs" did not run away, but instead came closer to the car. This is when I realized that these were not dogs — they were way too big to be domesticated dogs or coyotes, and they definitely were not wearing tags! After I drove by, the animals started following the car, not at an alarming speed. These beings were too massive to be dogs and had fur of snowy white with piercing eyes. I turned the car around down the road a bit, after I finally recovered from the shock of what I just had witnessed. As I was going back toward Ledyard on Lantern Hill Road, I did not see them again.

A year later, again in the fall, I happened to be back on Lantern Hill Road, accidentally getting lost heading home from Mystic. I realized what road I was on when I came to a clearing with a large pond next to it, exactly where I had turned around a year earlier. At this time, I commented to my traveling companion that we were on the same road as we were the previous year and we recalled what we had seen. No sooner than that, in almost exactly the same location, we spotted a wolf again, hovering around a mailbox at the foot of a driveway on the right hand side of the road, a little before Abbey's Lantern Hill Inn. It looked the same as the previous year, a large build with a white coat. Being skeptical as I tend to be, I was trying to look for a logical explanation. Again, I thought that these were huskies or coyotes, but the build was too massive to be a husky and way too tall to be a coyote. They could have been a hybrid: part dog and part wolf. As I was researching for

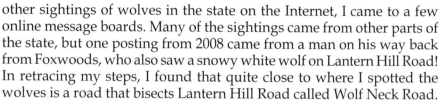

other sightings of wolves in the state on the Internet, I came to a few online message boards. Many of the sightings came from other parts of the state, but one posting from 2008 came from a man on his way back from Foxwoods, who also saw a snowy white wolf on Lantern Hill Road! In retracing my steps, I found that quite close to where I spotted the wolves is a road that bisects Lantern Hill Road called Wolf Neck Road.

Israel Putnam was able to alleviate the Connecticut colonists' wolf problem, but today, even though the state department may disagree, they are back, lurking in the wilds of the state.

Conclusion

Thank you all for accompanying me on this "off-kilter" journey through the Nutmeg State! We have met unique individuals, visited specialized museums, and have even seen a ghost or two. As you can see, Connecticut is certainly full of surprises! This little state has much to offer the visitor and the local alike.

Bibliography

Abrahamsson, Fay. "Camp Hadar Back in Spotlight," *New London Day.* (March 18, 2010).

Anastos, Leah. "Daniel's Village," *The Hartford Times.* (August 14, 1972).

Bayles, Richard M. *History of Windham County, Connecticut: Biographical Sketch of Israel Putnam.* (New York: W.W. Preston & Co., 1899).

Belanger, Jeff. *Encyclopedia of Haunted Places: Ghostly Locales From Around the World.* (Franklin Lakes, NJ: The Career Press, 2005).

Bell, Michael and Diane B. Mayerfield. *Time and the Land: The Story of Mine Hill.* (Roxbury Land Trust and Yale School of Forestry, 1982).

Bloom, Lary. "The Sun Sets on the Sunrise Resort," *New York Times.* (September 19, 2008).

Bowles, Adam. "Preston, Utopia to Hammer Out Details of Deal." *Norwich Bulletin.* (March 25, 2005)

Bradley Playhouse 2010 Theatre Season Program Guide. "About the Bradley History.," 2010.

Burr, George Lincoln. ed. *Narratives of the Witchcraft Cases: 1648-1706 Volume 15.* (New York: Charles Scribner's Sons, 1914).

Burr, George Lincoln. *New England's Place in the History of Witchcraft.* (Worcester, MA: Davis Press, 1911).

Campbell, Susan and Bill Heald. *Connecticut Curiosities.* (Guilford, CT: Globe Pequot Press, 2002).

Carini, Esta. *The Mentally Ill in Connecticut: Changing Patterns of Care and the Evolution of Psychiatric Nursing, 1636-1972.* (Hartford : Department of Mental Health, 1974).

Carroll, Michael C. *Lab Two Fifty-Seven.* (New York: Harper Collins, 2004).

CBS News Sunday Morning Episode 91. "Segment: Ellis Ruley." 1995.

Charles, Eleanor and Carolyn Battista. "Connecticut Guide," *New York Times.* (September 11, 1988).

Churaevka Historical Marker. "Russian Village: A Brief History."

Citro, Joseph A. *Passing Strange: True Tales of New England Hauntings and Horrors.* (New York City: Mariner Books, 1997).

Citro, Joseph A. *Weird New England.* (New York City: Sterling Publishing Company, Inc., 2005).

Clark, Marlene. "December 4 Will Mark 116th Anniversary Of Train Wreck." *Hartford Courant.* (November 28, 2007).

Connecticut Department of Environmental Protection. *Dinosaur State Park* brochure. (Newington, CT: Wolf ColorPrint, 2001).

Conspiracy Theory With Jesse Ventura Television Show. "Season Two, Episode One: Plum Island." (October 15, 2010).

Coolidge, Natalie. "Daniel's Village: A 19th Century Ghost Town." Killingly Historical Journal Vol. 2, No. 1. (1996).

Craven, James. "Norwich Plans to Restore Statue.," *Norwich Bulletin.* (October 18, 2011).

D'Agostino, Thomas. *Abandoned Villages in New England.* (Atglen, PA: Schiffer Publishing Ltd., 2008).

Deetz, James and Edwin S. Dethlefsen. "Death's Head, Cherub, Urn and Willow." *Material Culture Studies.* (Lanham, MD: AltaMira Press, 1999).

Dopirak Jr., William J., Associate Professor of Science at Three Rivers Community College and Gungywamp Society member, an interview by Zachary Lamothe, Groton, Connecticut, October 22, 2011.

Fitzpatrick, Jackie. "The Long-Lost Art of Ellis Ruley." *New York Times.* (April 21, 1996).

Friend, Tad. "The Nut Lady Returns." *The New Yorker.* (April 18, 2005).

Green, Pat, Bradley Playhouse theater manager, an interview by Linda Lamothe, Putnam, Connecticut. October 27, 2011.

Grigg, Bob. "Bob Grigg's Bytes of History: Winsted Wildman," *Colebrook Historical Society.* Available (Online) www.colebrookhistoricalsociety.org.

Harwell, Andrei. "Churaevka: A Russian Village in the Connecticut Woods.," *Russian Life Magazine.* (July 1, 2007).

Hesselberg, Erik. "Moodus Noises Strike Again." *Hartford Courant.* (March 24, 2011).

Hicks, Jonathan P. "Grand Met To Buy Nabisco's Heublein.," *The New York Times.* (January 17, 1987).

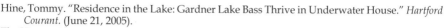

Hine, Tommy. "Residence in the Lake: Gardner Lake Bass Thrive in Underwater House." *Hartford Courant.* (June 21, 2005).

The History Channel. *Who Really Discovered America?* (A&E Home Video, DVD Release Date April 26, 2011).

Holtz, Jeff. "Mohegan Buy Rock Sacred To Tribe." *New York Times.* (July 8, 2007).

Jameson, W.C. *Buried Treasures of New England.* (Little Rock, AR: August House Publishers, 2005).

Kent, Donna. *Ghost Stories and Legends of Eastern Connecticut: Lore, Mysteries and Secrets Revealed.* (Charleston, SC: Haunted America, 2007).

Laschever, Barnett D. and Andi Marie Cantele. *Connecticut: An Explorer's Guide.* (Woodstock, VT: Countryman Press, 2006).

(The) Last Green Valley. *The Last Green Valley Presents: A Selection of Historical Characters: Notable and Notorious.* (Chicopee, MA: AM Lithography, 2008).

(The) Last Green Valley. *Walktober Brochure.* 2011.

Marcus, Jon. *Unknown New England.* (Bloomington, IN: 1st Books, 2003)

Marteka, Peter. "Former Sunrise Resort Losing Ground to Forest." *Hartford Courant.* (May 28, 2010).

Marteka, Peter. "Dip Your Tootsies Into Diana's Pool" *Hartford Courant.* (June 15, 2008).

Martin, Dr. Morgan. Former Superintendent of the Norwich State Hospital, an interview by Zachary Lamothe, Mystic, Connecticut, March 28th 2004.

Mccabe, Francis. "History Exhumed In Norwichtown." *Norwich Bulletin.*

Monagan, Charles. *Connecticut Icons: Symbols of the Nutmeg State.* (Guilford, CT: Globe Pequot Press, 2007).

"The Moodus Noises Renewed." *New York Times.* (October 23, 1888).

"New Insane Hospital Turned Over To State." *Norwich Bulletin.* (December 9, 1904).

"Ledyard Glacial Park." *New London Day.* (June 27, 2011).

"Norwich Man Collects Nearly Everything.," *The Hour.* (May 9, 1986).

O'Shea, Jim. "Connecticut's Castle Redux." *Hartford Courant.* (June 16, 2002).

Palmer, Michelle. *Gingerbread Gems of Willimantic, Connecticut.* (Atglen, PA: Schiffer Publishing Ltd., 2007).

Palmer-Skok, Viriginia. *Southbury Revisited.* (Charleston, SC: Arcadia Publishing, 2005).

Phillips, David E. *Legendary Connecticut: Traditional Tales From the Nutmeg State.* (Willimantic, CT: Curbstone Press, 1992).

Purdy, Stephen L. "The View From/Hartford; The History of Insanity, Shameful to Treatable." *The New York Times.* (September 20, 1998).

Pynchon, W.H.C. *The Connecticut Quarterly Volume Four: The Black Dog.* (Hartford, CT: George C. Atwell, 1898).

Report of the Killingly Historic District Study Committee regarding the establishment of Stone Road as a local Historic Property in the town of Killingly.

Revai, Cheri. *Haunted Connecticut.* (Mechanicsburg, PA: Stackpole Books, 2006).

Rierden, Andi. "A Steady Observer For Trembling Moodus." *New York Times* (August 6, 1989).

Rozhon, Tracie. "'For Sale' Sign Up at Connecticut Tourist Village." *New York Times.* (June 5, 1994).

Roxbury Land Trust. *Mine Hill: A National Historic Landmark.* (Roxbury Land Trust, 2007).

Skinner, Charles M. *Myths And Legends of Our Own Land.* (Philadelphia: J.B. Lippincott Company, 1896).

Stanley, Bill. "A Memorial Project for Norwich." *The Nine-Mile Square.* (Norwich, CT: Norwich Historical Society, 2005).

Stone, William L. *Uncas and Miantonomoh: A Historical Discourse.* (New York: Dayton and Newman, 1842).

Sullivan, Walter. "Connecticut Tremblors Defy Research On Cause," *New York Times.* (May 22, 1988).

USSVI-Memorial Committee. *US Submarine Veterans of WWII National Memorial East.* Groton, CT.

Wentworth, Alice. Former tour guide at Gillette Castle, an interview by Zachary Lamothe, via email, March 22, 2005.

"Will Save the State $56,100 Per Year." *Norwich Bulletin.* (March 23, 1901).

The Windham Textile & History Museum. *The Mill Museum and Visitor's Center Brochure.* Willimantic, CT

Woodside, Christine. "The Nut Lady Believed It Was Art. Now, a College Agrees." *New York Times.* (August, 4, 2002).

Zielbauer, Paul. "A Hill Full of Statues, but No Tax Exemption." *New York Times.* (December 8, 2000).